PERCEPTIONS OF TEACHING

Other titles in the Cassell Education series:

Perceptions of Teaching

Primary School Teachers in England and France

Patricia Broadfoot and *Marilyn Osborn*
with Michel Gilly and Arlette Bûcher

CASSELL

Cassell
Villiers House
41/47 Strand
London WC2N 5JE

387 Park Avenue South
New York
NY 10016-8810

First published 1993

British Library Cataloguing-in-Publication Data
A catalogue record for this book is available from the British Library.

ISBN 0-304-32773-5

Typeset by Colset Private Limited, Singapore
Printed and bound in Great Britain by Bookcraft (Bath) Ltd

Contents

Acknowledgements

The research reported here was funded by the Economic and Social Reseach Council whose support is gratefully acknowledged.

We should particularly like to thank the heads and teachers of the primary schools of Avon and Bouches-du-Rhône who gave up their time to fill in a daunting question-naire and, in some cases, to allow us into their schools and classrooms for two weeks at a time. We are also grateful to the education officials in the two countries who helped to facilitate access to the schools.

Among the many staff and students in the School of Education, University of Bristol, who helped in some way with the project, we should particularly like to thank Sue Cottrell, the project secretary and unrecognized research assistant, who returned from her new post to mastermind the manuscript for this book. Sheila Taylor and Anne Mallitte also typed drafts of chapters and helped in many ways.

We are grateful also to Valerie Houltom, who was an invaluable help and source of strength in the classroom studies stage of the project, and to Enid Buck, who assisted her in France. In addition our appreciation and thanks go to Sally Barnes and Oz Osborn, who provided constant support and advice with computing and statistical analysis.

Finally, we should like to thank Lucile Ducroqet, who undertook much of the transla-tion work.

Introduction

Over the past ten years education systems in many countries of the developed world have experienced an almost unprecedented crisis of confidence. There is a widespread belief that the level of illiteracy is exceptionally high, and that the younger generation is generally ill-equipped in terms of both knowledge and know-how for the demands of the world of work and the modern economy. Despite the evidence provided by steadily increasing success rates in public examinations that, contrary to popular belief, the average level of achievement reached by young people has been steadily rising, the anxieties persist. Part of the reason may be the ever-present fear of unemployment, which has led parents to become more and more concerned with the performance of their children at school, as well as the choice of curriculum options offered and the way in which these affect future career prospects. Another reason may lie in the fact that provision in a number of areas of the curriculum has not kept pace with current technological needs so that many employers are having to organize appropriate training for 'qualified' school leavers. Furthermore, it remains true that despite the various measures taken to remedy the situation, social class still remains a decisive factor as regards the scholastic achievement of pupils, and that children from disadvantaged backgrounds do tend to become the lowest achievers and the first to join the ranks of the unemployed. Given these persistent problems, teachers too are asking more and more questions regarding the nature of their professional objectives, and the best way to achieve these.

It is important to emphasize, however, that these fundamental questions concerning the quality and content of schooling are not a novel phenomenon. There have always been politicians, teachers and parents expressing concerns about the extent to which schools are actually meeting the current needs of our society. Since provision for mass education began to be made towards the end of the nineteenth century, reflecting and encouraging the rapid growth of industrial societies, the various questions asked have become more and more pressing, more and more complex. In consequence, educational provision has been a constantly changing landscape.

In the two countries with which this study is concerned – France and England – there have been many recent expressions of educational changes which have been brought about by concerns regarding the content, quality and accountability of schooling. These have focused particularly on curriculum content and new approaches to teaching and school organization. But in the mid-1980s, when this study was conducted, such changes relating to teaching content and practices had in no way affected the more fundamental characteristics of educational provision or the characteristic national practices of the two educational systems involved. The French educational system was (and moreover still is) a centralized system, the organization of the schools, the curriculum and the various responsibilities of teachers and other staff having been established at national level. The enforcement of the various national directives was the responsibility of a number of hierarchically organized bodies: the Rectorats, the Inspections Académiques and the Inspections Départementales. In England, by contrast, the educational system was very decentralized, the responsibilities regarding school staff and curriculum being mostly within the control of the local authorities. The decisions taken had of course to conform to overall ministerial policy, but the autonomy of the schools was a defining characteristic of the system. Put crudely, it was possible to contrast one system with a 'vertical' structure and a powerful hierarchy, with a concentration of the power at the top of the hierarchy (the Ministry), with the other, more 'horizontal' system characterized by a weak hierarchy, and a high degree of decentralization so that much of the power was traditionally vested in the local authorities and the schools themselves.

It is because the two educational systems were organized in such radically different ways that the authors of the present book decided to undertake the research presented here. The comparison between the two systems seemed all the more important and useful since, as early as 1985, discussions and arguments in the area of education allowed us to anticipate that the basic principles underlying both these very different educational systems would soon be the object of radical rethinking for the first time since the beginning of the century. Given that the underlying principles of the educational system are likely to shape in a very clear fashion the day-to-day running of schools, and also the conception that the teachers have of their role and their responsibilities, it was important to examine any differences in the relationship between policy and practice in two such different systems before important changes actually occurred.

The changes which are being implemented in the early 1990s in the two countries are indeed of a new kind in so far as they relate to the most fundamental features of the two educational systems. These changes are actually a reversal of the basic principles described above. In France, the emphasis is now on decentralization and a greater measure of autonomy for individual schools; in England, the emphasis is on centralization and the compulsory application of national directives. The 1988 Education Reform Act means that primary and secondary schools in England now have to follow a National Curriculum, and the level of the pupils will now be assessed according to national norms. The considerable degree of autonomy enjoyed hitherto by English schools is being reviewed, and the power of the local authorities is being drastically reduced.

In France, the 1988 Jospin law sees the beginning of more autonomous and outward-looking schools as it sets up school projects involving all of the people who have an interest in education, and who are directly concerned with the cultural, social and economic interests of the local community. The curriculum is to be seen only as 'the framework around which the teachers will organize their teaching'. The 1988 law therefore gives much more responsibility to the local level; it also gives more autonomy to the individual schools, and places the official seal of approval on the practical involvement of local bodies in the school system. Given the nature of the French educational system, this is indeed a radical change. Through the granting of more initiative to the bottom of the hierarchical structure, the Jospin law aims to bring about a substantial degree of decentralization, whilst the Education Reform Act in England with its National Curriculum and assessments places more emphasis on national directives and centralized power.

Our research was carried out before the above changes actually took place, at a time when the two educational systems were still based on fundamentally different principles, in two countries with very different cultural traditions. It therefore had as a first, central objective questions concerning the relative importance of systemic variations for educational delivery. Building on an earlier, more limited comparative study (Broadfoot, 1981), the aim was to ascertain in a systematic fashion to what extent it is true that particular institutional systems, together with the cultural traditions from which they derive, represent a major influence on teaching practices and on the conception that teachers have of their role and responsibilities.

To sharpen the international comparisons, the research also set out to explore the relative significance of more local sources of variation, notably the geographical location of the schools within the same country, as judged according to the social make-up of the area. The importance of such local variations is emphasized in the work of Bourdieu and Passeron (1977) in France and Sharp and Green (1975) in England among many others, in which it is argued that social class influences both teachers' objectives and their practice. The study of Isambert-Jamati (1984) also confirms that primary teachers' practice differs according to the social composition of the pupils concerned.

To the extent that it exists, the influence of the socio-economic location of the school can be explained in different ways. These include: teachers' working conditions; pupil characteristics; parental expectations and support; teachers' prejudice and motivation, plus specific directives and constraints emanating from within the institutional system itself.

Thus the comparative perspective used in this study was a double one – *inter*-country and *intra*-country – and has a dual interest. The first goal was to be able to compare the effects of *inter*-cultural differences linked to the history and structure of the two systems to the effects of *intra*-cultural differences linked to differences in organization and delivery of the two systems according to the local populations concerned. This comparison allowed us to evaluate the relative importance of the two major sources of external constraints: those which relate to the common objectives and ways of functioning of each of the national education systems in general and those which relate to the particular local work conditions influencing individual teachers and schools. But this double comparison has a further element of interest in the possible interaction between the two major sources of difference. Thus we were able to consider whether the effect of the particular socio-economic location of a school was of the same order in the two countries and, by contrast, whether the impact of the national system was similar in different types of local area.

The first objective of our study was therefore to compare the importance of two key external factors – the national context and the local environment – on teachers' views about their work and their professional obligations. It was not our only objective. At a time when the institutional changes mentioned above were starting to take shape, it was also our objective to offer some preliminary insights concerning the potential significance of such changes for educational practice in the two countries. In particular we wished to study the way in which these changes were likely to affect teachers' practices and professional conceptions. Given that since the beginning of our study the two systems have started, in a more or less clear-cut fashion, to evolve in opposite directions, it would seem appropriate to monitor how far teachers in the two countries are becoming more similar in their approach to their work. In this respect the systematic comparison carried out before those changes actually took place is most useful, as the basis for future comparisons.

Before turning explicitly to these questions, however, we conclude this introduction with a brief outline of the book as a whole. In addition to Chapter 1, which elaborates in more detail the rationale for our study, Part I includes brief descriptions of the evolution of the educational systems of the two countries with which we are concerned and provides a brief account of current arrangements in the provision of primary schooling in England and France. In so doing we hope to provide some general contextual background against which the reader can interpret the more detailed analyses that follow. Chapter 4 explains how our enquiry was conducted and should thus provide readers with the detail they need to assess the credibility of our findings.

The remaining chapters of our report are divided into two further parts. Part II, comprising Chapters 5 and 6, is concerned with factual details about teachers and their work environment as provided by our respondents in their questionnaire responses. These two chapters provide a picture of the objective contrasts between primary teachers themselves in the two countries and of the working conditions they experience in school.

Part III, by contrast, explores the second set of influences on practice as we have identified them in this chapter – the interpretations of their professional obligations and responsibilities held by the teachers themselves. In Chapters 7 to 10 we explore the way in which teachers define the task of teaching, their aims and their frustrations, their freedoms and their perceived constraints which combine to determine their day-to-day practice in the classroom.

We shall comment on and discuss the differences noted as they are presented. This will therefore enable us to see a number of general characteristics, whose main features will be discussed fully in our final chapter, both from the point of view of their theoretical and of their practical implications. This chapter also provides a summary of the differences described in preceding chapters and attempts to draw out both the theoretical insights to be gained from such comparisons and their practical implications for future action within the two systems.

Part I

The Background

Chapter 1

Teaching and Society

Teaching lies at the heart of the educational enterprise. It is the point of delivery of the education system and the key to its success. Because of this, teaching is the focus for numerous research projects and the subject of constant debate. The abiding concern of policy-makers and researchers is to understand better the nature of teaching in order that a better learning environment can be created. Although any teaching–learning relationship will be defined by certain constant features that relate to the nature of the task itself, each teaching–learning situation will also be influenced by a range of contextual influences such as the age of the pupils, how many there are and their motivation for being there. It is relativities such as these in the teaching situation which help to determine both the kind of pedagogical approach that can be employed and also the objectives which are being pursued. The search for quality in teaching is conducted in a context where theoretical absolutes must give way to the compromises of politics and the realities of the possible.

Within the familiar web of constraints that influence the nature and hence the quality of teaching, we may distinguish two main elements. The first consists of those essentially external factors which impinge on teachers. These will include the ideological traditions and administrative arrangements of the national education system, its changing policy priorities and resourcing; it will also include provision for training and professional activity within the system, and the impact of the institutional context itself and the more subtle influence of parents and the local community.

The second, very general element of influence on teaching comprises factors which are essentially internal to the teacher herself.* Such factors will include the teacher's skill and commitment, ideology and personality, which combine to make up the teacher's professional persona. These two sources of influence on teachers combine to determine the nature of their professional practice. They also determine the scope for change and the way in which this may best be brought about. To understand the way in which teachers respond to the different influences upon them is thus to discover the key to the effective implementation of policy changes. Despite the apparent simplicity of this model, policy-makers have typically shown little awareness of the need to go beyond

---

*To avoid excessive use of 'he or she', etc. throughout the text, 'she' is used to refer in a general sense to a teacher, and 'he' is used to refer to a pupil.

ministerial fiat to bring about change. Disregarding Crozier's (1964) classic statement 'on ne change pas la société par décret', policy-makers have tended to concentrate upon directives concerned with the first set of influences defined above – those external to the teacher – and have arguably neglected to address the potentially powerful role of teachers' personal ideology and skill in determining what they do. How significant these relative sources of influence are is therefore an important empirical question in the overall pursuit of educational quality. The relative effectiveness of bureaucratic directive as against attempts to bring about change by working through the perceptions of teachers ought to be a key focus for educational enquiry. It follows from this too that mechanisms for ensuring that the quality of *existing* educational arrangements, as well as potential new initiatives, ought to be subject to the same questions. Is it external inspection, direction and control that is most likely to ensure commitment to the education system's goals and standards? Or is it teachers' own sense of moral responsibility – to themselves, to colleagues and, above all, to their pupils – which is the more powerful motivating force?

These vital questions constitute the core of the study we report in this volume. Prompted by the findings of an earlier study (Broadfoot, 1981) which revealed unexpected and significant differences in teachers' approaches to their classroom practice in the very different education systems of England and France, we set out to discover the sources of influence on teachers' conceptions of their role in these two countries. Commonly regarded as classic examples of centralized and decentralized systems respectively, whilst being in many other respects broadly similar, France and England were chosen as countries where differences between the power of external constraints as against internal influences on practice would be likely to be thrown into the sharpest possible relief.

The strength of this substantive national comparison was further reinforced by the adoption of a combination of sociological and psychological approaches. The traditionally rather reductionist sociological concern with the relative power of a variety of external forces both to determine policy and to impact on practice was combined with the psychologists' concern to clarify the relationship between teaching and society as this is effected in the minds of teachers.

Thus the object of the research was to go beyond the formal and explicit differences enshrined in legal statutes and contracts to the actual perspectives held by individual teachers which give meaning to their actions and now, in particular, govern their responses to the 'reformitis' (Weiler, 1988) being brought about by the speed and scale of social change.

This rapid social change is currently posing fundamental questions for many societies about what should be the nature and purpose of education. Such questions embrace not only the obvious issues of what needs to be learned, to what level and by whom, but also equally important concerns about the delivery, organization and structure of such provision within the over-arching debate between education as public investment and education as personal enrichment. It is these policy dilemmas which lend a particular cogency to our research. They emphasize the subservience of all educational endeavours to the priorities of a particular time and place. They remind us that the goals of education, as well as the means, are fundamentally social in character as Durkheim (1956) pointed out at the start of the twentieth century. A similar point is made by Acker (1987):

> The content of what is to be learned; the conditions under which the encounter takes place;
> the characteristics of the parties concerned all reflect the social and cultural arrangements
> of a given society in a particular era . . .

The history of subsequent decades has borne witness to Durkheim's assertion. For the greater part of this century, politicians, planners and researchers have been pre-occupied with questions of educational provision. Concerns about social justice, national development and the need to identify individual differences have also domi-nated the sociological and psychological research agendas in education. In so doing both disciplines have tended to disregard the potential significance of the teaching context itself.

In recent years, however, there has been a radical change in this respect. The common ground between psychological and sociological perspectives has come increasingly to the fore in studies of classroom processes informed by symbolic interactionist and phenomenological perspectives. Studies in the field of metacognition in psychology have increasingly stressed the importance of understanding how learning takes place and what contextual factors may influence this. At the same time, structuralist, neo-Marxist, macrosociological accounts stressing the economic determinants of education have given way in the sociology of education to more dialectical accounts which seek to relate consciousness and context in a strategic way. In particular, attention is increas-ingly being focused on teachers and how they resolve the diverse pressures upon them in terms of action.

It is this more recent perspective we have sought to build upon in our research. Our aim is to add to the considerable body of recent research which has begun to explore the significance of teachers' thinking and how their view of professionalism informs their classroom actions and is in turn related to the context of their lives as a whole.

> Alongside this recognition of the complexity of the teacher's task and the importance of the interplay between initiating and responsive acts in the classroom, greater attention has been directed to teachers as human beings, as rounded social actors with their own problems and perspectives, making careers, struggling to achieve their ideals or just struggling to 'survive'.
>
> (Ball and Goodson, 1985, p. 8)

COMPARATIVE PERSPECTIVES ON TEACHING

A still more recent development in the combined efforts of sociologists and psycholo-gists to understand the complex nature of the educational process is the recognition that international comparisons have a particular role to play in highlighting some of the major determinants of teachers' practice. Such comparisons make possible a study of the way in which particular national traditions and social settings can influence how the task of teaching is seen.

> Teaching can be seen as a task or a role, performed with others; as a profession or career; as an activity shaped by historical, social and economic forces. . . . Thus the work of the primary teacher, however concentrated on day-to-day roles and relationships, cannot escape the influence of social, economic and political change. These factors by no means determine her every move, but provide the context and constraints within which she makes her choices and finds her satisfaction.
>
> (Acker, 1987)

Recognition of the potential role comparative studies can play in illuminating action as well as system, process as well as structure, has been an equally recent phenomenon. The traditional emphasis in the field of comparative education on either analyses at the level of policy and provision or of single country studies has only recently been recognized by calls for more interactionist and case study accounts (e.g. Broadfoot, 1977; Crossley and Vulliamy, 1984) which can compare the subjective realities of different populations and use these as the basis for generating new conceptual frameworks through which to analyse education.

In particular it has been the very evident common problems with which educational systems in many parts of the world have recently had to grapple which have underlined the logic of such an approach. Rapid technological change and financial cut-backs have combined in many countries both to pose new challenges to schools and to decrease their capacity to meet them. The result in many countries has been a lowering of teacher morale, innovation fatigue and retreat into routinized practice (Webb and Ashton, 1987), which may reduce stress but also reduces teachers' capacity to respond positively to changing educational needs.

Studies such as those of Poppleton (1990) and the international Teacher Satisfaction Study network provide good examples in this respect. These studies reveal constant features of job satisfaction across the countries studied, such as good teacher–pupil relations, and also important differences which have their roots in the ideological and cultural traditions of the individual societies in question. Thus, for example, where teachers in both England and the USA place great emphasis on professional autonomy as a source of job satisfaction, this is not so elsewhere. Stress, which correlates negatively with job satisfaction in England, is positively correlated with job satisfaction in Japan (Menlo and Poppleton, 1990).

Studies of this kind can thus raise important questions to challenge ethnocentric assumptions about cause and effect. For instance, Poppleton (1986) found that in England, job satisfaction is a function of perceived reward whereas ratings for work centrality and stress are a function of an individual's values; such findings are illustrative of the kind of theoretical development that such international studies make possible, helping us to develop not only greater insight into the specific differences between teachers in the countries studied but also more sophisticated analytical frameworks through which we can interpret these differences. The increasing concern among educational researchers with substantive issues of educational policy and practice has been prompted by the accelerating rate of social change. This concern has in turn tended to erode the boundaries between disciplinary enclaves which were formerly characteristic of educational research. Sociologists and psychologists, comparativists and philosophers have begun to find common cause in their efforts to elucidate key operational concepts such as professionalism or accountability.

The study reported here is an example of this kind of approach. Prompted by major changes in both French and English educational policy in the current decade, which are having the effect of moving both systems away from tradition and closer to each other, the research has brought together both sociological and psychological perspectives in a comparative study that seeks to address the origins of such changes and their implications for teaching. More fundamental still is the intention to use this same comparative psychosociological perspective to explore the influences and constraints which determine how teachers perceive their professional role.

It was hoped that the use of the comparative context in particular would allow us to distinguish those aspects of teachers' professionalism which are constant in any classroom situation, such as the need to direct learning, to have good relationships with pupils and to control pupil behaviour, and those aspects which are the product of a range of situational variables, such as the institutional context, cultural traditions, bureaucratic structures and national policy.

The pursuit of such distinctions is not merely an academic nicety. It is fundamental to the effective formulation and implementation of educational policy. Without reliable evidence about the relative significance of different sources of influence upon teachers' conceptions of their professional responsibility, it is impossible for policy-makers and administrators to judge the likely impact of particular policy initiatives or indeed to run the education system on a day-to-day basis in the most effective way.

SOCIOLOGICAL PERSPECTIVES ON TEACHING

The responsibility of central government for the formulation of educational policy and for the overall imposition of a system of provision makes international system comparisons an obvious focus for any study of variations in teachers' conceptions of their role. However, this level of analysis needs to be complemented by an attempt to address other external and systematic sources of influence on teachers. In particular, a long history of sociological interest in equality of educational opportunity testifies to the significance of major intra-national differences for the way in which teachers see and carry out their role. The work of, for example, Bourdieu and Passeron (1977) and Isambert-Jamati (1984) in France and of Sharp and Green (1975) in England suggests that pupils' perceived home background characteristics may exercise a substantial influence on both the goals that teachers identify in relation to *particular* pupils and how they set out to achieve these in the classroom. To the extent that this is so, differences in the socio-economic location of individual schools will interact with more general national differences either to intensify or to weaken the overall patterns of difference. Thus despite the profound importance of different national traditions and arrangements, it is possible that there may be more similarity between teachers working in the same type of local socio-economic circumstances in two different countries than between teachers working in very different local conditions within the same national setting.

Any attempt to analyse the relative importance of different structural constraints on teachers' conceptions of their professional responsibility must therefore address a range of contextual factors which logic and existing research both suggest will exert related but diverse influences on those conceptions.

PSYCHOLOGICAL PERSPECTIVES ON TEACHING

Such sociological modes of analysis do not, however, take into account more micro-level sources of variation which are associated with the teacher herself, rather than the context. Among such variables might be included the age and sex of the teacher, his or her training, experience and current post – all of which are objectively classifiable variables which can further contribute to the construction of interactive matrices for explaining variations in teachers' professional priorities.

But although a study of the relative significance of variables of this kind can provide a useful map of the factors at work, it is weak in explanatory power. It cannot account for the relative importance of various sources of influence nor describe how these are articulated in the minds of teachers. And yet the most salient reality about teaching is the way in which the individual teacher reconciles a host of external influences and constraints with more or less personal views of her role which emanate from her own biography and personality on the one hand and the inter-personal situation she may find herself in at any one time, on the other. Where the politician is charged with formulating the broad strands of policy, and the academic with analysing different aspects of its application in practice, the teacher must act, must solve in the best way she can the diverse dilemmas posed by the interaction of personal goals and external constraints, and of professional priorities and individual needs.

As an increasingly substantial literature on teacher strategies (Woods, 1986) and teachers' thinking (Calderhead, 1987) illustrates, both the conception and the act of teaching represent a complex process of mediation between subjective and objective reality which is expressed in the form of particular representations (Gilly, 1989) of the task in question. Thus to understand fully the significance of variations in the teaching context at national, local, institutional and personal levels for the formulation of particular versions of professionality it is necessary to address the subjectivities of teachers and the processes by which such variations take on particular significance in the working life of the teacher. In particular it is such subjectivities that are the key to understanding teachers' responses to change in some aspects of their working environment, whether this is a minor change in school organization or a major change of direction initiated at national level.

We deliberately chose to emphasize the teachers' conception of their role and the external factors that might affect this conception. It is clear that teaching practices are affected by a body of external constraints (directives, working conditions, etc.), in the same way that the practices of any other profession are. And the influence of these constraints can be assessed directly, without recourse to the teachers' opinions of what they do. Such studies are useful, but they do miss out one important element in the understanding of the way teachers work, and of the difficulties involved in attempting to get them to adopt different practices. It is a fact that when considering the way individuals function within society, the relationship between external constraints and practices is not a straightforward one, since it involves the mental conceptions which individuals employ in order to decide on, and to justify, their professional behaviour. These conceptions may include personal factors related to the characteristics of each individual, to their life history, and to their own individual experience. But for the most part, because such conceptions are those of individuals who all belong to the same group, with identical positions in society and similar interests, they are to a large degree similar. To put things succinctly, the conceptions of the job and of the role depend upon social representations of the job which, as well as being useful for deciding on and justifying professional practices, also serve as a common set of group-defining characteristics shared by all the individuals who have those representations. Does the fact that the teachers are English instead of French, or work in disadvantaged areas rather than in middle-class areas, affect the view that teachers have of their job? Whether this is so will depend on the relative impact of these two external sources of influence on the practice itself.

As we shall see in the first two chapters, the differences between the two school systems (English and French) were such at the time of our study that it seemed reasonable to assume that the influence of the general way in which each system was organized would be rather greater than the influence of the sociological characteristics of the specific location of the schools. In other words, our general hypothesis was that differences would be greater between countries than within the same country in different areas with regard to teachers' conceptions of their role, the teaching practices and their view of professional responsibility. With reference to the theory of social representations such a hypothesis corresponds to what we know about relationships between ideologies, practices and social representations (Gilly, 1980, 1989). Although the question has not been definitely answered, several works do show that effective practices can play a major role in the construction of, and changes in, social representations.

We shall adopt the view here that the general ideologies (of a social kind) underlying the institutional systems have a relationship with the representations (of a psychosocial kind) shared by the various members of that particular institution only if they imply clear differences in the particular practices of those members. In the situation with which we are concerned, the structural differences between the two systems (which follow from different ideologies and cultures) would seem to be more likely to affect teaching practices than the differences connected to different working conditions within the same country. As we shall see in Chapter 3, this particular way of looking at the problem implied that the teachers should be asked questions regarding both their actual working conditions and teaching practices, and the conceptions they have of their role and of their responsibilities.

THE PROBLEMS OF CHANGE

France

The salience of this argument is well illustrated by recent research findings in both France and England which highlight just how little impact some efforts at reform initiated at national level have had. Anxious to remove some of the worst inefficiencies of the almost overwhelming inertia created by the sheer size of the centrally run French education system, the government has engaged in a series of policy initiatives. These are aimed at 'deconcentrating' some administrative responsibilities and 'devolving' a greater measure of autonomy for decision-making to local authorities and even to the hitherto almost completely powerless headteachers. The degree of success so far achieved testifies to the inadequacy of change emanating from bureaucratic directive alone.

> 'We've been trying to get more flexibility into the system for 10 years, but no one will let us', says M. Delaquis, the French deputy chief inspector. 'Everyone believes that you must have the same programmes, the same number of hours devoted to subjects, the same kinds of textbooks, the same training for teachers . . . a common programme is integral to the concept of equality of opportunity. It's entrenched by history. It's natural.'
> (TES, 6.3.87, p. 19)

> as an exasperated Minister of National Education, René Monory, recently exclaimed in the Assemblée Nationale, 'In this country, as soon as you touch a single comma in education, you have a revolution on your hands!'
> (Weiler, 1988, p. 252)

One of the reasons France is trying to introduce more flexibility into the system is because it has proved very difficult to adapt the education system to meet the new demands now facing it. The impact of youth unemployment, changing technologies and consequently greater demand for vocational training in schools has been matched by the social and political pressures for equality of opportunity and thus for educational provision to be seen to be meeting the needs of the majority, rather than just the traditional academic elite.

Ways are therefore being sought of encouraging flexibility and creativity among the teaching profession by loosening at least to some extent the traditional monolith of bureaucratic accountability. Yet there is compelling evidence that such attempts have so far met with little success. The analysis of Valérie Isambert-Jamati (1984) reveals that, despite the scale of these reforms, the lack of any corresponding change in teacher attitudes and, in particular, of their representations of their professional role has led to the perpetuation of an educational system in which the teachers are still the main perpetrators of elitism and educational failure among particular social groups. This argument, which was first put by Durkheim in the early part of the twentieth century and reiterated by Bourdieu and Passeron (1977) and which is still being reiterated in more recent studies, points to the neglect by change agents of the need to address teachers' ideas if any fundamental change of direction is to be achieved.

The relatively recent LeGrand reforms on secondary education provide continuing testimony in this respect. In an attempt to help schools and teachers meet the needs of the increasing numbers of pupils who are ill prepared by their family life and social circumstances, LeGrand recommended that greater pastoral provision be made in schools and, in particular, that a tutorial system should be established. Teachers' reaction to the report was hostile and highly selective. The report was seen as posing a challenge both to their conceptions of their professional role and, more practically, in terms of potentially longer hours and in demanding a range of skills which were not those they associated with teaching.

These examples are typical of repeated attempts by French education policy-makers to transform an education system whose deeply rooted traditionalism is inhibiting its ability to meet the needs of a society undergoing rapid social change. This is largely as a result of opposition by the teachers themselves. A substantial popular literature on the current 'crisis' in French schools testifies to the tensions that are created when attempts to change the content and delivery of education are not accompanied by opportunities for both teachers and consumers to work through the issues for themselves and so evolve the new understanding which will in turn inform the necessary changes in ideology.

England

In England, the same emphasis merely on changing structures rather than recognizing the need to change attitudes as well has also been strongly in evidence in recent policy initiatives. Instead of seeking to identify what are likely to be the most effective ways of influencing what teachers do, policy has increasingly been based on the premise that perceived public and industrial concern over educational standards and the content of the curriculum can be most effectively dealt with by centrally inspired measures designed to limit teachers' autonomy. In particular, the economic recession of recent years and an associated backlash of public concern over supposedly falling standards have led to a notable 'tightening of the reins' and an upsurge of interest in the notion of accountability, particularly in its crude bureaucratic form of 'calling to account'.

The confidence in education which characterized the days of heavy investment in human capital has been steadily eroded by years of economic recession and associated educational scapegoating, and has been increasingly replaced by coercive and punitive attempts to ensure value for money through a whole range of assessment measures.

With the onset of the present decade, it is clear that central government has come to appreciate the power of assessment techniques to give teeth to curriculum exhortations. As Hargreaves (1988) suggests, there has been a move from an era of policy-making in which the predominant concern was with the administration and reorganization of educational provision through a decade or more when the focus was on curriculum change in favour now of an explicit emphasis on assessment and appraisal. Thus the 1988 Education Reform Act provides for national assessments in key subjects for all pupils at ages 7, 11, 14 and 16 as part of the new National Curriculum.

Coupled with the institution of 'teacher appraisal' and strategies aimed at giving central government a good deal of the financial control hitherto exercised by local authorities, it is quite clear that government in England is engaged on a pattern of educational policy-making which assumes that tighter control will lead to a more efficient, homogeneous and productive education system.

It is clear from these examples drawn from both England and France that governments will seek to impose perceived national priorities on the education system. Indeed, this must necessarily be the *raison d'être* of any *national* education system. However, it is also clear, even from these very brief examples, that the nature of the priorities identified will, in turn, tend to dictate the strategies chosen for bringing about the desired changes. It is at this level that policies can so easily be rendered impotent if they do not take into account the factors that determine the behaviour of those charged with the responsibility of putting policy into practice, namely the teachers.

Indeed, it is not always easy to alter the practices of a profession. At the present time many teachers in France and England are worried, and rather reluctant to adopt the changes proposed. This is due to the fact that by nature the relationship between institutional systems, practices and individual conceptions of a role is rather complex. The fact is that the 'hard core' (Abric, 1984) around which such conceptions are organized gives these representations a great deal of inertia. When confronted with the uncertainties and radical rethinking which characterize any time of change, this inertia means that stable referents which give a sense of security can be preserved, so that individuals are able to retain their sense of worth, and their mental equilibrium. It is not surprising therefore that the changes in practice demanded by the reform of the system should come up against, to a greater or lesser degree, and for a variable period of time, already existing role conceptions, and, in particular, certain central aspects of the way in which people see their role and their professional responsibilities. Hence the usefulness of a proper understanding of the role conceptions of the members of the group, which in turn allows for a proper understanding of the reasons why people are reluctant to accept the changes in their practices required by institutional reform.

THE RESEARCH STUDY

Thus the starting point for our research was to question prevailing assumptions about the nature of educational control and to seek instead to establish the relative significance of various sources of influence on teachers' practice. Findings from a previous project (Broadfoot, 1981) had established that there is a complex interrelationship between formal organization, institutional and ideological traditions and contemporary pressures on the education system. Of particular note in this respect was the earlier finding that because of the near impossibility, given the contemporary size of the educational industry, of effectively controlling the educational process itself through detailed monitoring and sanctions, teachers in France in many ways enjoyed considerably more freedom from external pressure than their English counterparts, who lack the protection of central civil servant status against local pressures and who are subject to constant evaluation in terms of the results of their pupils.

Paradoxically it was found too that French teachers' ideological commitment to centralization as the basis for equality of provision and their tradition of formal powerlessness means that they rarely challenge the taken-for-granted conceptions of their role to make use of this freedom. This is in sharp contrast to England, where such autonomy is a central tenet of professional ideology. Put another way, this means that there is a need to look at the embodiment of diverse sources of influence and control in the way teachers see and carry out their job, in their notions of professional responsibility.

A broader term than accountability, the concept of responsibility, is much better able to embrace the notion of self-imposed priorities, which is clearly an important dimension in any profession where self-imposed goals and standards of conduct provide, through self-regulation, one of the most significant influences on practice. McIntyre (1977) elucidates this responsibility clearly in defining five different levels of a teacher's endeavour to which it may apply. Although acceptance of responsibility in terms of a given criterion does not imply a willingness to be accountable to others in terms of that criterion, it is a necessary condition for such accountability. Morrison and McIntyre (1975) suggest that teachers' conceptions of their responsibility are in terms of criteria which teachers *plan* to meet and on which they are prepared to *evaluate* their teaching. They suggest five 'levels of responsibility' may be identified:

1. aspects of the teacher's own activities;
2. pupils' overt classroom behaviours;
3. pupils' mental experiences during classroom activities;
4. pupils' attainment;
5. pupils' typical future behaviour.

Acceptance of each level necessarily involves those preceding it. Teachers can only realistically take responsibility up to the second or perhaps third level. Problems may arise when interested parties such as parents or higher educational authorities hold unrealistic expectations of teacher responsibility or are unwilling to provide the freedom or the facilities for teachers to achieve that for which they are held responsible.

In what follows we explore teachers' own perceptions of the influences on their practice; the external and self-imposed constraints within which they must work and the nature and effects of such obligations and constraints. In particular we examine how much scope for personal initiative and autonomy in deciding and implementing pedagogic and policy objectives is enjoyed by teachers in the two countries. The discussion is structured in terms of three different levels of analysis: empirical questions, theoretical questions and practical questions. The first level is essentially descriptive and involves reporting the differences between the two national groups of teachers studied which were identifiable from the data in terms of four key questions:

1. In what ways do French and English primary school teachers differ in the way they conceive of their professional responsibilities?
2. How much do variations in the social context of teaching *within* a particular national system affect these national patterns/stereotypes?
3. What is the source of any such difference?
4. What are the main sources of influence which affect how teachers see their professional responsibility?

The second, more theoretical set of questions builds on the first in an attempt to understand the salience of the differences themselves and the sources of those differences as they were identified:

1. What is the significance for the teachers themselves, their pupils, and the success of the education system as a whole of variations in teachers' views of their professional role?
    (a) The policies and administrative arrangements of the national education system within which they work?
    (b) Other less informal influences such as professional associations or parents' wishes?
    (c) The imperatives of classroom and institutional life as embodied in the task of teaching a large group of children?
    (d) The teacher's own personality, experience and training as embodied in her personal ideology?
2. How may such 'professional' responsibility best be conceptualized?
3. What implications do such analyses have for efforts to identify any absolute determinants of 'good' teaching?
4. What is the potential contribution of comparative studies of this kind to the development of insights about how change in education is accomplished?

The third and final set of questions concerns the practical implications of the findings of the study:

1. What effect are the major policy changes currently being introduced into both countries likely to have in the light of the answers to questions 1–3 above?
2. Are there optimal strategies that should be employed to realize the goal of changing teachers' practice?
3. How can educational quality best be promoted?

Our overall conclusions will be concerned with whether there are indeed the systematic differences in how the professional role is viewed that the formal differences in organization and ethos of the two systems would suggest, or whether there are other, systematic sources of influence which are more powerful in determining what teachers think and do.

The scale of the differences which emerge in this respect in relation to the two national groups is remarkable, given the proximity of the two countries. This in itself reinforces the importance of our enquiry and validates the logic on which it is based. It is this logic that we have attempted to describe in this chapter. Why these differences should exist and what significance they hold at a time when both countries are introducing substantial changes which will move them away from their deep-rooted traditions and towards a common middle-ground, are questions we address in Chapter 11, which forms the conclusion to the book. Whilst we could not have anticipated the timeliness of the results of our enquiry when it was initiated in 1984, it seems likely that our conclusions will be of considerable relevance to the successful pursuit of today's major policy initiatives.

Chapter 2

A Historical Overview of the Primary Schools in France and England

English and French schools today are still very much a product of their respective national traditions. Although English primary schools may appear very different today from those of thirty years ago, the underlying principles informing the structure and organization of primary schools have changed relatively little. In the case of French primary schools this is still more true, it being commonly agreed that today's primary school is demonstrably similar to that introduced by Jules Ferry in 1882.

Both educational systems remain marked by the tremendous industrial, economic and social changes that characterized the nineteenth century. Both in France and in England, the emphasis was on the urgent need to set up a basic school system for the masses. However, the particular school systems that developed in both countries were different: their history is a reflection of the historical development of the individual country. It is well known that the 1789 French Revolution, 'which was fought in order to control the school system, rather than to transform it' (Furet and Ozouf, 1977), shaped the whole of the French school system. Schools were no longer under the control of the Church, but under that of the State, and they were spread evenly all over the country, with no fees to be paid. In England, the lack of such a dramatic historical event allowed for the spread of independent schools and a more gradual move towards State-provided education.

Although in France the Revolution and the idea of identical elementary schools for all led to the creation of a national system, in England the existence of a national school system is much less obvious, given the degree of autonomy allowed to teachers in the area of school syllabuses and the level of independent responsibility traditionally held by local authorities. It is these fundamental differences in approach between the two systems which represent the core of our study and the key to understanding its significance. In this chapter and the next, therefore, we shall look first at the various stages which characterized the historical development of both educational systems and then describe both systems as they were in 1984, at the beginning of our study.

THE FRENCH PRIMARY SCHOOL SYSTEM

The French educational system is currently the subject of a debate. Parents and teachers are questioning both its objectives and its organization. Following consultations that took place in January 1989 between the Ministry of Education and teachers' and parents' associations, the educational law of July 1989 outlined a new look for the education system.

In order to combat academic failure, the plan was to give a greater degree of autonomy to the schools, and to encourage teachers to get involved in extracurricular activities. The salary of teachers would no longer depend exclusively on experience, but also on other criteria such as working conditions and teachers' involvement in the whole educational process. Finally, there was to be greater involvement of parents and the local community in education though teachers would still retain their main responsibility for the transfer of knowledge.

These changes in French education proposed under the 1989 law are not in the same league as the upheavals associated with the Education Reform Act of 1988 for the English school system. But the French law, which aimed to 'develop, organize and modernize the educational system', opened up new perspectives, and gave new objectives to both primary and secondary schools, with a view to 'enabling all pupils to acquire a diploma'. For 65 per cent of the school population, this diploma was to be the 18 + *baccalauréat*, with the remaining 35 per cent being expected to acquire a professional qualification. This goal alone implied far-reaching changes, given that in 1988, according to Institut National de la Statistique et des Études Économiques figures, only 36 per cent of the relevant cohort passed the *baccalauréat* (general, technological or professional), and that 12 per cent of pupils left school with no qualification.

To understand fully the significance of these contemporary developments it is necessary to put this in a historical perspective and to go back to the roots of the education system itself. At the end of the nineteenth century, the Third Republic established a system of primary schools intended for the masses. The primary school system was run totally independently from the rest of the educational system, and led, for more than half a century, to the *certificat de fin d'études primaires* (CEP). Only the selected few could go on to study for the *baccalauréat*. The 1989 educational law, however, aims to ensure that all children acquire either the *baccalauréat* or a professional qualification. The aim is no longer, as it was in the nineteenth century, to eradicate illiteracy, but rather to ensure that everyone is educated to a high standard. In 1989, 20 per cent of the school population entering secondary school had difficulty handling their own language. Thus the role of the primary school, where children learn to read and write, is being brought sharply into focus.

In documenting the changing shape of French primary education three important landmarks will stand out as most significant. These are:

- the 1789 Revolution, with its three important notions of equality of access, independence from the Church, and absence of fees;
- the Ferry laws (1881–90), which mark the end of a century of struggle during a politically very unstable time;
- the 1959 bill, which makes attendance at school compulsory for all children under the age of 16, and which sets up the system of 'Collèges d'Enseignement Secondaire' in order to satisfy the overwhelming demand for a democratization of the school system.

Before we can expand on these three stages, however, we need to discuss briefly the pre-1789 period. It is a fact that, although the 1789 Revolution was a vital stage in the establishment of a primary school system for all children, it did not actually invent this system.

The origins of the French primary school system

The primary school system was not set up at the time of the Revolution, as it was already flourishing during the last century of the Monarchy. Schools were from the very beginning seen by the Catholic Church as an instrument for controlling the masses socially and intellectually.

(Furet and Ozouf, 1977)

Just before 1789, 'a mosaic of different institutions and practices, sometimes competing, sometimes complementary' (Furet and Ozouf, 1977) was spread unevenly over the country. The Church was the only body to take an interest in the education of the masses. Schools first started in towns, where they were set up near churches; in the country, their establishment was slower. The objectives of those schools were simple: reading was taught so that children could follow properly both mass and catechism.

The schoolteacher, under the control of the Church, was poorly paid, and often exercised other functions within the parish, as well as having another trade. Was the schoolteacher in those days a real teacher? She or he had to live by a strict moral and religious code, and was not allowed to attend balls or go to the café. After the proclamation of the first Republic in 1792, the State delegated responsibility for primary schools to the local authorities. However, this decision was not accompanied by any financial measures which would have made its implementation possible. No new teachers were trained, with the result that the clergy quickly regained their leading position in the schools. It was therefore much more a case of maintaining the old school system than creating a totally new system.

It was another century before a school system totally independent from the Church was created. But as early as 1835 Guizot was laying the foundations of the current primary school system. It was the local council's duty to create a school which would remain under the control of the mayor and other important citizens. Guizot made it compulsory for the local councils to pay primary school teachers a fixed salary, which would be on top of the pupils' families' contributions. Fifty years later, these contributions were scrapped in favour of a State-paid salary. However, this idea of a salary paid for by the State and not by the children's families was already present in the Guizot bill. The fixed salary paid by the local councils was regularly increased throughout the nineteenth century. For Duruy, free schooling was essential, both to avoid competition between schools, and to allow for a democratization of education.

The Guizot law of 1835 set up the primary school inspectorate whose function it was to keep an eye on primary schools. The Falloux law of 1850 set up the primary school inspectorate at the level of the *département*, whose function it was to keep a list of primary school teachers for the benefit of the local councils who could then select their own teachers. Even though the local mayor and other important citizens still tried to keep a degree of control on primary schools, the setting up of this particular body means that the schools were independent regarding educational matters. 'A gradual emancipation of the school administration takes place' (Prost, 1968, p. 93).

The question of the training of schoolteachers had already been looked at by Guizot.

He had planned one men's teacher training college for each *département*, which would be responsible for the training of primary school teachers. It was not until Duruy, who became Minister for Education in 1863, that the importance of training female primary school teachers was understood. Teacher training colleges became coeducational only very recently (1975).

Throughout the nineteenth century the number of primary schools continued to increase, the idea of free schooling became established, and the fixed salary paid by the local councils got bigger. In 1863 Duruy sought to develop a primary school system which would be free and compulsory. He set up vocational training for future workers as a separate strand from the rest of the educational system. This was to remain a characteristic of the educational system until the second half of the twentieth century.

During the latter part of the nineteenth century, scientific and technical advances, and further industrialization meant that education for all became as much an economic necessity as a collective idea. The laws of Jules Ferry (1881–83) relating to primary schools were more a recognition of an already existing state of affairs than a true upheaval.

The historical development of primary schools between 1789 and 1881 definitively shaped the system at the national, regional and local levels. 'In the end,' as Prost (1968) says: 'the primary school system can therefore be defined as a public service at the level of the *département*, which makes use of buildings belonging to the local authorities, and has teachers who are employees of the State'.

One of the direct consequences of free schooling was the notion that primary schools were a public service. As early as 1889, primary school teachers became State employees: their salaries were paid by the State.

The laws of Jules Ferry

The Ferry laws, which represent the culmination of a century of struggles, laid permanently the foundations of the French primary school. The three fundamental principles that date back to the Revolution are maintained, and in fact they are still valid today: schooling was to be compulsory, free, and independent from the Church. For instance, the 1967 guide for primary school teachers says that 'the method to be adopted in primary schools was first defined by the Instructions of 1887, and still remains fully valid nowadays.'

Schooling became compulsory for all children of both sexes between the ages of 6 and 12. All towns and parishes had to open a boys' school and a girls' school. (Schools only became coeducational after 1968, although there were exceptions to this rule in isolated areas where two different schools would have been too costly to run.) It was not until the Popular Front of 1936 that schooling became compulsory up to the age of 14. Compulsory schooling up to the age of 16 was brought about by the Berthoin decree of 1956. The decision at a national level to make it compulsory for parents to send their children to school was indicative of a new way of thinking. Until then, it was compulsory merely for towns and parishes to open a primary school. Parents were free to decide whether or not to send their children to school.

In due course the primary school was charged with another obligation – the establishment of a final exam: the CEP (*certificat de fin d'études primaires*), which marked the end of primary school education. The idea for this exam, which gave an independent aim to primary schools, dates back to Guizot in 1834. With its very own diploma, the primary school was independent from the rest of the educational system.

Thus, primary schools were set up to be a secular, public service, and reflected the essential ideology of the republican movement, based as it was on equality and the right to education for everyone. The Ferry laws established the educational system as a legal obligation, and Jules Ferry makes a clear distinction between the public domain (the law), and the private domain (conscience). He saw the State as responsible for teaching, with religious education being the responsibility of individual families.

Those laws, which date back to the end of the nineteenth century (1881–89), represent the foundations of the primary school. They covered every single relevant area, whether it was timetables, syllabuses or teaching methods, for several generations of primary school teachers, and they constituted the fundamental body of rules regarding primary schools. Thus, the primary school which was established in 1881 remained in the same form for a long time although there were a number of other developments which modified primary schools somewhat. In 1923, the official instructions from Paul Lapie relating to teaching methods emphasized the need for progression in the syllabus, and advised teachers to avoid repeating the same elements from one year to the next. In 1945, the syllabus was trimmed. These official directives, however, did not attempt to modify the objectives of the primary school defined in 1881. Such modification occurred only in 1975, with the Haby bill.

It was also at the end of the nineteenth century, at the same time as the shaping of the primary school took place, that the first teacher union appeared. From the outset, this union was a power to reckon with, and had two important characteristics: it had a large number of female members, and a clear intention to be close to workers' unions. Although these teachers' unions changed noticeably, their role has always been important. Union representatives are present in a consultative role in most technical commissions at the national, regional and local levels. These commissions deal with staffing (appointments, promotions, etc.) and posts (creation and closure of classes, schools, etc.).

Twentieth-century reforms

Two other attempts at reforming the educational system took place after the fundamental laws of 1881–86. In 1936, Jean Zay, who was the Minister for Education, put forward a bill which made schooling compulsory up to the age of 14. This bill proposed the introduction of a common core for all children between the ages of 11 and 14. Although the bill did not succeed, the democratization of secondary education had been started. After the Second World War, the Langevin–Wallon bill, inspired by emerging research on child psychology, introduced the notion of a single type of school, and suggested new teaching methods. Once again, the bill was unsuccessful. Both these projects, however, even though they did not materialize, played a part in the destabilization of the education system, and more particularly, of the primary school system. There was a growing demand for a better education at grass roots level, and the proportion of working-class children entering secondary education gradually increased. On the other hand, in the middle of the twentieth century, the economic landscape was rapidly changing. There was a need for different and better qualifications for workers; the CEP had become inadequate. Both economic and social reasons were fuelling the need for change in the education system.

The ordinance of 1959 represented the next major step in the transformation of the primary school. This law, which made schooling compulsory up to the age of 16 and did away with the entrance exam for the first year at secondary school, meant that the primary school had to modify its objectives, and that the secondary schools had to become more democratic. Financial constraints, however, delayed this reform and it made very slow progress, becoming totally effective only in 1975 with the Haby law.

From 1959, all children could hope to enter secondary school. This in turn led to both qualitative and quantitative changes in secondary schools. It quickly became apparent that there was a need for many more classes for the new pupils. The CES (*collèges d'enseignement secondaire*) were created to cater for the first four years of secondary school; the secondary school, which until then had catered for an elite, now had to provide for the masses.

The old CEP classes disappeared only very gradually. It was not until the introduction of the Haby law that these classes finally disappeared. From 1975 onwards, all children entered a common secondary school. The objectives of the team who drafted the 1975 bill and introduced compulsory schooling up to the age of 16 were to create the possibility for all children to fulfil their potential, to become educated, to become good citizens, and to be well equipped for entry into active life. All children were to start school at the age of 6. Primary school consisted of five years organized as three successive cycles: preparatory, elementary and final, leading to entry into secondary schools.

The 1975 bill also included another aspect of democratization: it gave parents some say in the running of the schools. This, however, was only very tentative and in no way stands up to comparison with the English school system. Up to 1975, teachers had to meet three times a year. Nowadays, there is also a committee made up of parent representatives, and a school committee made up of teachers and parent representatives. This school committee cannot influence teaching methods, as this area is still the exclusive responsibility of teachers, who follow official directives. The committee's only function is to deal with practical questions (such as special events, maintenance of the school buildings, extracurricular activities, etc.) which do not involve teaching methods or the contents of the syllabus.

The Haby reforms were only partially successful in overturning entrenched professional attitudes and methods, as in, for example, the practice of repeating the year. When Jean-Paul Chevènement replaced Alain Savary as Minister of Education in 1984 he brought a return to an emphasis on education for national development and moved away from the preoccupation with promoting greater equality in education which had prevailed in the preceding decade. The educational history of the first part of the 1980s is essentially one of turmoil, with every level of the education system first coming under detailed scrutiny by a major national commission and then being the subject of more or less substantial proposals for change. This turmoil was a reflection that the national consensus which had for so long informed French education had largely disappeared in the face of rapid and major social change. It was also a reflection of the difficulty of making any attempt at change effective.

Despite these difficulties and as a result of the continuing concerns at national level to bring about change within the education system, in 1989 the Education Minister, Lionel Jospin, introduced new legislation which was designed to bring about a radical alteration in some of the most cherished traditions of the educational system.

1989 and the 'loi d'orientation'

The changes proposed by the 'loi d'orientation' affect the very structures of the educational system. As we have seen, the French educational system is organized according to a vertical structure, the decisions being taken at the national level, and implemented at the local level under the supervision of school inspectors. With the new system, these national directives make up the framework within which each primary school, each CES and each *lycée* will work out its *own* policy and practice. These policies, which are specific to each school, have a dynamic function, and are meant to breathe new life into the system. They must take into account the various social and cultural characteristics of the area that each school serves. Moreover, they require the active participation of everyone who has a direct interest in education, such as teachers, parents and pupils, and of the other bodies concerned in the running of the schools including associations and local councils. The principle of partnership is established, and extracurricular activities, which must complement the academic activities, rather than replace them, must form part of those policies. The changes being brought in by the 'loi d'orientation' are therefore fundamental to the extent that there is now more autonomy for teachers and schools. Finally, extra financial aid in specific areas will be available to schools. Although this new autonomy for teachers and schools is the main characteristic of the new law, two other aspects seem equally important, namely the evaluation of the educational system, and teacher training.

The setting up of a national committee for the evaluation of the educational system at all levels is a totally new concept in France. Up until now it was only exams such as the *brevet élémentaire* and the *baccalauréat* which had an evaluative function. The fact is that although the main objective of these exams is to assess the pupils, they can also be used to perform an evaluation of the quality of the educational system. With this new reform, teaching quality will be evaluated and rendered public through the publication of annual reports.

Finally, this new law provides for *instituts universitaires de formation des maîtres* (i.e. training colleges at university level) to be set up which will replace the old Écoles Normales, and will train primary and secondary school teachers. Moreover, teacher training will now involve many different professions: not only academics, researchers, teachers, inspectors and educational advisers, but also doctors, economists and various other professions will all participate. Here again, we may anticipate fundamental changes given that until now universities had nothing to do with teacher training. A large degree of autonomy will be granted to the teacher trainers, who, although they will fit in with a national framework, will also have a great deal of freedom as regards the selection of the staff involved and of certain parts of the courses. The changes are part of the new national policy of decentralization. Although the school system as a whole will still be administered at national level, the new importance given to teachers and schools is likely to result in significant changes in both the attitudes and the practices of teachers.

THE ENGLISH PRIMARY SCHOOL SYSTEM

In recent years English primary schools have attracted considerable international attention as pioneers of child-centred approaches to education. Within the context of considerable autonomy for local education authorities (LEAs), schools and individual teachers, novel approaches to classroom organization, curriculum planning and teaching methods have evolved on a scale which makes the average primary school now unrecognizable compared to those which previous generations attended. Such developments have not been without opposition from those favouring more formal educational arrangements, and recent years have seen an increasing level of controversy in this respect leading to calls for greater accountability for schools and teachers and tighter central control. These tensions have now culminated in the imposition, from 1988, of a National Curriculum and assessment framework to cover the whole period of compulsory schooling. This unprecedented step in the history of English schooling throws into stark relief the various currents of development which have characterized primary education since the late nineteenth century.

In the brief résumé that follows, these historical themes are set against the rapidly changing arrangements that are currently impacting on primary schools in order to provide some insight into the context which underlies the analyses of subsequent chapters.

The origins of the English primary school system

Arrangements for mass educational provision in England and Wales (Scotland and the other parts of the United Kingdom have separate systems; see Bell and Grant, 1974) have frequently been characterized as 'a national system, locally administered'. Other commentators would go further and dispute whether, traditionally, public educational provision merited the description educational 'system' at all since for most of its history, mass educational provision has been a local responsibility with only the most basic requirements being laid down at national level. One of the reasons for this was the existence of powerful entrenched interests in the great variety of provision that evolved to provide elementary education in the eighteenth and nineteenth centuries.

Unlike France, where the Revolution and subsequent Napoleonic era had led to a formal national commitment to a unified system of provision, the lack of an equivalent watershed in England allowed the independent growth of Church schools, 'dame schools' and a range of other private and charity establishments to flourish as well as the widespread practice of employing governesses and tutors in the home.

As the nineteenth century progressed, however, it became increasingly apparent that voluntary agencies and in particular the Church could no longer provide schooling on the scale necessary to train and control the masses for the new industrial society. It was necessary both that the State should provide at least an elementary education for the masses in order that they should acquire both relevant skills and appropriate work and social disciplines, and that the State should be able to control the amount and content of schooling according to the needs of the economy and the funds available.

In 1861 the Newcastle Commission on Popular Education in England was set up to examine the current state of mass educational provision in England and to consider what measures, if any, were needed for the extension of sound and cheap elementary 'Instruction to all Classes of the People'. Although this Commission recommended some State funding to support elementary schools, it was not until 1870 that the Forster Education Act introduced the concept of State-provided elementary schools to fill any gaps in existing voluntary-aided provision of schools and provision for compulsory attendance. In 1880 the Mundella Education Act made elementary education compulsory for 5–10-year-olds.

This brief account serves to highlight how the important differences in the management of educational provision in England and France, already enshrined by the turn of the century, were crucial in determining the emerging power structures in education and the characteristic ways in which the basis for either conflict or consensus between interest groups was created.

But although this was arguably the beginnings of a form of education system in the latter half of the nineteenth century, the power of local interests (Simon, 1965) and an ideology of grass roots autonomy which was already deeply rooted in English institutional history meant that central control of the English education system – if it existed at all – had to be largely informal (Johnson, 1980).

Thus as Archer (1979) points out, the establishment of a legal basis of a system for mass educational provision in 1870 was more an act of recognition of the steadily increasing, if diverse, local provision for education that was being made through Boards of Education, the Church and charity schools, than the result of any very deliberate attempt to create such a system. Thus the creation of an education system in England had little to do with the imposition of a central bureaucracy as in France and a great deal more to do with broad national policies and a framework for inspection, monitoring and assessment to ensure minimal standards of provision.

Her Majesty's Inspectorate (HMI) was set up in 1840 as the first national machinery for evaluating and influencing schools (Silver, 1979). The function of these Inspectors was both to disseminate good practice and to provide information for government on the state of the nation's schools; they were a 'communication system between government and its main educational agency on the one hand and the schools for which they provided support on the other hand' (Silver, 1979, p. 5). Unlike their French counterparts, they did not have inspection of individual teachers as part of their brief.

More explicit testimony to the importance of assessment in controlling the emergent education system was provided by the Revised Code of 1862, which soon became known as the 'payment by results' system. The Revised Code offered each school a block grant based on a common formula – a system designed to cope with the rapid expansion of elementary school provision that was then taking place.

The principles of the Revised Code corresponded exactly to the cost-effectiveness principles characteristic of business at that time. The system required the overall level of school grants – from which teachers were paid – to be dependent on the proficiency of individual children in meeting the standards laid down for the various grades. The effect of the Code, which was to encourage drilling, rote-learning and frequent testing in the three Rs, to the exclusion of almost every other aspect of the curriculum, academic or social, lasted for generations.

In 1867 it became possible under the Code of Regulations governing elementary schools to add other subjects to the original standard subjects so that by the 1890s the number of subjects had greatly increased (Simon, 1965). Teachers were given 'guides' rather than set books. The Cross Commission, which reported in 1888, was particularly important in this respect. This was also the beginning of the Higher Grade Schools and with it the first attempts to provide 'secondary' education for the masses in a system which would be parallel to, but separate from, existing elite provision. By 1895 the system was already crumbling, so that by 1907 the curriculum was open to a measure of negotiation between teachers and HMI to the extent that the 1911 Schools Board Report shows an increasing difference in provision for different schools, areas and sexes (Eaglesham, 1956).

It can be seen that the imperatives of maintaining public order, responding to industrial change and concern for social justice which led in England in the nineteenth century to the introduction of mass compulsory education at least partly funded by the State and with a centrally prescribed curriculum, were very similar to those in France. The tension between Church and State in struggling for control of that provision, the explicit separation of mass elementary education from the emerging secondary provision for the middle classes, and the lowly status of elementary school teachers were all characteristic of both countries' educational provision during the second half of the nineteenth century. At the same time, the distinctive characteristics of both systems were already in evidence – the French with an elaborate framework of centrally imposed organization and State-employed teachers, the English authorities already placing great emphasis on using various forms of evaluation to ensure some degree of common standards in a network of locally provided schools over which they had little direct jurisdiction.

Other administrative and professional developments in the education system at this time also encouraged this distinctively English approach to educational provision. Critical in this respect was the growth of teacher unionization, local authority power and public examinations. These three developments were closely related.

The growth of teacher unionism may be seen as directly related to the 'payment by results' system and one cause of its decline. The National Union of Elementary Teachers was founded in 1870, the same year as the major Education Act introducing universal elementary education, arguably because it was already apparent that the real power in elementary education was the State and not the (local) School Boards.

The 1902 Education Act, which created a new system of School Boards and significantly expanded the scholarship ladder to fee-paying secondary education by creating local authority secondary schools, helped to fuel the growth of teacher unions as it meant that elementary schools became increasingly irrelevant to mainstream provision, one effect of which was to allow elementary teachers considerable autonomy.

The curriculum reorganization introduced by Robert Morant between 1903 and 1905 provides another example of the approach to managing national educational provision which had already become a characteristic feature of the system in England by the turn of the century. This reform was explicitly designed to stop elementary schools developing in a secondary direction since it excluded secondary-type subjects, such as science, from the permitted curriculum.

In England, moreover, the monitoring of educational activity, the flow of information within the system, became a key element in system accountability and, hence, control. The institution of national commissions became a characteristic feature of the decentralized English system in which government, both local and central, depended upon such information to provide for its own accountability to electors and hence for its own policy-making, in contrast to France where tight central control of all ingredients in the educational process, notably resources, management and curriculum, made it more possible for government to take for granted the nature and quality of educational activity.

The scholarship examination, initially introduced to ensure that the introduction of free places in secondary schools 'shall not have the effect of lowering the standard of education provided by the school' (Board of Education, 1906, p. 67; quoted by Sutherland, 1977) rapidly became highly competitive and marked the beginning of a stranglehold on primary school teaching and curriculum which would be exerted by competitive secondary school selection until the introduction of comprehensive secondary schools in the mid-1960s.

Public examinations

Public examinations were also of great importance in this respect since the pressure to gain such qualifications was highly instrumental in ensuring the efficient functioning of schools. Scholarship examinations to select children from public elementary schools for secondary school scholarships were instituted at the same time as universal State provision of elementary education in 1870. This route was greatly expanded after the 1902 creation of local authority secondary schools and the Free Place Regulations of 1907, which required grant-aided (i.e. partially State-supported) secondary schools to offer a quarter of their places to elementary (i.e. State) school pupils (Sutherland, 1977).

When Selby-Bigge asserted in 1927 on behalf of the Board of Education that 'we must look to examinations rather than inspection to check, test and secure the efficiency of public education' (Silver, 1979), he summed up the emerging character of the English educational tradition very well.

Development in the mid-twentieth century

Thus historical circumstances, informed by deep-rooted cultural traditions, led central government in England and Wales into being largely unwilling, as well as unable, to attempt a highly bureaucratized, centrally controlled education system like that of France. A thumbnail sketch of the essential aspects of English educational provision as it evolved during the twentieth century would reveal a system still dominated by the nineteenth-century legacy of the struggles between rival groups for control over the emerging educational system, a struggle which gave rise to an anarchic 'ideology of teacher autonomy and governmental interference as a monstrous entity to be resisted at all costs – a situation in which central government was typically happy to concur' (Salter and Tapper, 1981).

The 1944 Education Act, which was a milestone in the development of educational provision by making secondary education for all both free and compulsory, nevertheless continued this tradition by imposing on local authorities the statutory responsibility for the running, staffing and teaching of its schools. Only the broad framework of a tripartite system of provision based on 11 + selection for grammar, technical or 'secondary modern' education and the laying down of an obligation for all schools to provide religious education – again a notable contrast with France – were the subject of central direction. The Act continued the tradition of an educational alliance between teachers and local authorities. In practice, a good deal of what was officially local authority responsibility devolved upon individual schools and headteachers.

There were, of course, inevitable limitations on teacher autonomy: the teacher–pupil ratio, the inability of most schools to choose their pupils, public expectation of appropriate teaching and moral rectitude, and external examinations. The curriculum equally was subject to a variety of influences, including HMI and local inspectors, subject associations, national statutory bodies, and standing Advisory Councils, as well as periodic government committee reports and the educational press. Nevertheless it is probably true to say that during the 1950s and 1960s the reality of teacher autonomy in practice approached more nearly to the prevailing ideology than it ever had before. The growing willingness to trust teachers' 'professionalism' which made possible this autonomy at the level of practice was also the basis for teachers to have a strong voice in policy-making at both local and national levels.

Thus for most of this century, apart from its minimal statutory obligations, as set out in the various Education Acts, the formal powers of the Department of Education and Science (DES) have been largely limited to the control of resources and the monitoring of local authority activity within the overall context of a particular value framework (David, 1977).

In practice, like the relations between local authorities and schools, centre–local relations have been a complex blend of advice, policy statements, encouragement, monitoring, provision and sanctions.

If in the 1950 and 1960s, decentralization meant, almost literally, the right for teachers in their classrooms to do what they wished without interference, increasingly it has come to mean 'the right to make decisions within an understood framework of operation'. As far as the curriculum is concerned, there has been a shift from the post-1944 situation, in which curriculum responsibility was delegated to headteachers, to a situation in which, following the issue of Government Circular 14 in 1977 which asked local authorities to describe the procedures which they had established for carrying out their responsibility for local curriculum provision, there are increasingly precise national requirements in every area of provision, backed up by an increased monitoring and inspection role of local advisers and inspectors.

Thus, the English system evolved from a variety of local initiatives, which themselves reflected a number of different political and social interests. Because of its pluralistic origins and the sometimes irreconcilable interests embodied in it, it has proved very difficult to lay down any direct control of education on a national basis. Instead, such control as has existed has been mediated through various kinds of examination and assessment procedures, which in themselves impose goals on the system, and, less obviously, through the imposition of a particular set of values and goals which become the focus for teachers' self-imposed responsibilities. Most significant in the latter respect have been Her Majesty's Inspectorate and various national commission reports. Furthermore, both consumers and administrators have a fairly clear idea about the limits of acceptable variation between schools, so that the freedom that does exist for heads and teachers to pursue their own objectives is, in practice, relatively limited.

Nevertheless, it remains true that, when compared to the French system, English primary school teachers have a quite remarkable degree of freedom to teach how they wish and what they wish. One of the most significant effects of these differences is the important role that the school as a unit has in England in the development of its own ethos and collegial and staff support systems, etc., as compared to France, where teachers are employed by the centre and see their allegiance as being primarily to the body which employs them, rather than the individual school. The significance of these differences for the way in which teachers conceive their professional responsibility will be apparent from the chapters which follow.

The Plowden era

In the 1960s primary schools began to be set free from the constraint of the 11+ selection examination for secondary schools through the introduction of comprehensive secondary schools. The Plowden Report of 1967, *Children and Their Primary Schools*, clearly expressed the prevailing conviction that schools could help to overcome social problems if teachers were allowed to exercise their professional judgement in relation to the needs and interests of the individual child (Becher and Maclure, 1978). The report argued strongly for child-centred primary education and gave a major impetus to the development of this ideology and practice among primary teachers. However, a series of critical publications issued shortly after the Plowden Report – the Black Papers (the first was Cox and Dyson, 1969) – bear ample testament to the concern among certain sections of society at this time, over the apparent movement away from traditional curricula, pedagogy, discipline and internal grading practices in schools in favour of teacher autonomy. This concern continued to increase during the 1970s and led to growing support for greater consistency of provision and, hence, central government control:

> During the 1970s, the DES assumed a much more assertive role in educational policy, in relation to partners in the educational alliance. . . . The contributions of non-governmental groups to the decision-making have been gradually restricted as the central government has sought to impose national goals upon the rest of the system
>
> (Litt and Parkinson, 1979, p. 15)

Recession and utilitarianism: the era of accountability

The speed and scale of the changes which took place in English education in the 1970s may be attributed to the concatenation of the two main causes of this change in the tide: the economic depression which set in in the early 1970s, and the changing style of government, at every level.

Since that time a series of government policy papers has laid down in increasing detail the priorities for education and a range of procedures to be followed. Teachers' pay bargaining rights have been withdrawn in favour of imposed rates of pay which are linked to staff appraisal procedures. At the same time the power of school governors has been substantially increased through a series of Educations Acts. The overall effect of recent changes has been to strengthen *both* central bureaucratic control and community influence on schools and teachers.

The Education Reform Act 1988

In 1988 this influence was formally incorporated into new powers of control on the part of central government. The Education Reform Bill, which became law in July 1988, gave the Secretary of State for Education approximately 220 new powers, notably in the areas of curriculum, assessment and finance. In broad terms the Act made all but the smallest primary schools responsible for their own budget and the governors of those schools responsible for every aspect of their functioning – educational and financial. Both primary and secondary schools are required to teach the National Curriculum, which is based on detailed programmes of study for defined 'core' and 'foundation' subjects. The pre-specified attainment targets in each of these subjects are the focus for a national assessment framework which incorporates formal assessment and reporting procedures at four 'key' stages: 7, 11, 14 and 16 years. The results are reported in detail to parents and aggregated across classes and schools for general publication in the form of increasingly notorious 'league tables'.

Thus the English education system is currently embroiled in changes more fundamental than almost any in its history. The power of LEAs – the traditional location of political, as well as of administrative, decisions about education – has been severely curtailed and replaced by wide-ranging central controls. At the same time provision within the Act for schools to opt out of local authority control, if the parents wish, may in time mean the end of a State-provided education *system* and a return to the great diversity of types of school – albeit still funded by the State – which prevailed prior to the introduction of mass elementary education in 1872.

CONCLUSIONS

In this chapter we have given a brief historical overview of the context in which primary schools were developed in France and England. The two systems are very different, and they have both been deeply marked by the political, economic and social history of Western Europe. The same significant events – the Reformation which followed the Middle Ages, the striving economy which characterized the nineteenth century, the deeply felt need for democratization which marked the 1950s, the opening of European frontiers which is happening today – all led to reforms and changes, some superficial, some fundamental. In fact, in both countries education became a subject of debate whenever economic and social changes demanded it. Moreover, those identical stages which feature in the development of the two school systems are comparable in that they reflect, in each case, both the demands of the economy and its requirement that schools should provide high-level training in new technologies, and the demands of a population with growing aspirations.

At the end of the Middle Ages, the problem of illiteracy affected the whole of Europe. In England in the sixteenth century, the victory of Protestantism, which led to the establishment of the Church of England, coincided with the birth of a new economy. The small schools which had been set up by the Church started to spread. In France, the reform of the Catholic Church, in reply to the Reformation, was also a feature of a society in evolution. Elementary schools, usually attached to individual parishes, were set up. In both countries there were close links between schools and the Church, and the objectives of the schools were both moral and religious. These small schools started spreading unevenly throughout the country, both in France and in England. The links between schools and the Church are still a feature of schools in England, whereas in France there is no longer any direct link between the two bodies. However, the presence of the Church is still felt in France, and quarrels between those who want the Church to be involved in the education system and those who do not are still very much alive.

The French Revolution saw the setting up of a national primary school system, a phenomenon which did not occur in England. In practice, however, another century was needed in both countries for schools to be established in every village and town.

In both countries, the nineteenth century was characterized by great industrial and social turmoil, and the need to educate all children, as well as to achieve moral control of the population. This meant that the State had to become involved. But when the two educational systems were set up at the end of the nineteenth century, although their objectives were similar, their characteristics were radically different, following the respective cultural traditions of the two countries. The French primary school system was set up as a public service, with the aim of civilizing the population. In England, there was no system as such, merely official recognition of the existing schools (set up either by the Church or by charitable organizations).

In England, the local authorities were responsible for deciding on the nature of the curriculum and on the organization of schools. The State subsidized but did not control. The nineteenth century saw the setting up of a 'system' where the State provided a framework within which the local authorities were in charge of the organization of schools and responsible for the curriculum and the teaching staff. However, a number of factors, including the expectations and pressures of the families, the role of specialist bodies, the existence of a public examination system, and constraints on staffing levels, always restricted this autonomy of the English schools system.

In France, the end of the nineteenth century saw the setting up of an educational system in the true sense of the word, where the State assumed power in the areas of curriculum design and organization of the schools from the local authorities and the Church. The advantage of the system is that the teachers are totally independent; they are State employees, and there is no possibility for pressure at the local level, as they are accountable only to the school inspectors. In England, teachers are not, and do not regard themselves as, State employees. In France, teachers are accountable to the State; in England, teachers are accountable to their own schools.

The French system is likely to continue to function in a remarkably stable fashion for a long time. The English system, on the other hand, is likely to continue to be more open to change. Hitherto the freedom available to schools and teachers meant that teaching practices could evolve according to current professional ideology and educational research. In many English primary schools a real revolution has taken place, so that the emphasis has switched from the traditional acquisition of knowledge through a pre-established syllabus and formal teaching to the acquisition of knowledge through a discovery process and re-experimentation. There is in France an interest in innovation in teaching, but it seems that the weight of the administration, both local and national, is such that change cannot readily take place. There is a fundamental contradiction here in the fact that French teachers on the one hand are handicapped by a lack of freedom because of the existence of a National Curriculum, and on the other wait for the blessing of the authorities before experimenting with, or applying, innovations. In the following chapters, and more particularly in Part III, we shall look at the impact of these historical traditions on the two school systems, and on what the teachers say regarding their teaching practices and their responsibilities.

The two educational systems are currently undergoing radical changes. In England it is possible to trace in current developments a clear move to emulate the practices of more centralized education systems like the French one, presumably in the hope of gaining their perceived advantages. However, there is no corresponding ideological rationale in a commitment to equality of opportunity, and national unity. Rather the inspiration in England is a novel one – it is that of the market and the combined application of standardized quality control procedures on the one hand and consumer preference on the other. The reader may well be able to draw some conclusions from the chapters that follow about the likely impact on teachers of this radical departure from English educational tradition and of the equally radical changes taking place in France in relation to that system. In both countries changing economic and demographic pressures appear to be leading to similar and novel techniques of control which combine a measure of local autonomy in the implementation of central directives with pervasive monitoring arrangements in the more general development of what Neave (1988) has called 'the new Evaluative state'.

In these brief historical accounts it is apparent that common social and economic imperatives have been mediated by national culture, politics and institutions into two very different systems of educational provision. As the countries of Europe move ever closer following the economic union of 1992 and in anticipation of future political union, it seems as if hitherto very different systems may be moving towards some optimum, common point between centralization and decentralization (Broadfoot, 1982a). More accurate, perhaps, is the view that the terms 'centralized' and 'decentralized' are no longer adequate to describe the new apparatus of control through a combination of financial provision and detailed monitoring which is now emerging (Broadfoot, 1983).

At the same time, the scope of educational provision is itself changing to embrace new populations – for example in the burgeoning pressure for the expansion of education and training post-16 – and it may well be that in both England and France, as elsewhere, the education system is poised for change on a scale similar to the reform that brought in mass elementary education at the end of the nineteenth century. Such changes will have their own administrative imperatives which we cannot as yet predict. However, an awareness that this is so will help to underline the point that the study reported here is only a snapshot in time of two constantly evolving systems, the different facets of which are more or less constant features but all of which are potentially open to change when social circumstances dictate. In the chapter that follows we develop this snapshot in outlining the current characteristics of primary provision in each of the two countries, and thus the specific working environments for the teachers who form the subjects of the study reported here.

Chapter 3

Primary Schools in France and England at the Time of Our Study

LIFE AT SCHOOL

School buildings

Both in France and in England there is a tremendous variety of school buildings, ranging from imposing old buildings to more modern designs characterized by space and light. School buildings are always designed along the same format: one classroom for each teacher. In England, however, many new schools have a rather more flexible layout which means that a number of classes can be regrouped in the same room, thus enabling teachers to organize group work easily. In England, school buildings always include a library for the pupils, an office for the head, and a staffroom. In France, however, until fairly recently there was no provision for an office for the school head. At the present time much effort is being put into improving the situation, so that staffrooms, multi-purpose rooms and libraries can be organized whenever space permits. Rooms in fact are often available for this purpose, following the decline in the birth rate. Finally, both countries have a national scheme which enables schools to acquire computer equipment. In fact, there are very few differences between British and French schools, at least from the outside. Inside school buildings, the situation is very different, as many examples of pupils' work can be found in English schools in entrance halls, corridors and classrooms. This is a very important difference between the two countries. In England, schoolchildren work in less strict and more friendly conditions. In the classrooms, the desks are very rarely lined up opposite the teacher's desk, and are instead arranged in small islands, thus allowing for group work. In most classrooms there is a water tap, a small library, and a rest area with cushions and carpets. Finally, in England the staffroom is a work room where meetings are held, as well as a coffee room; in France the staffroom, where it exists, is most often intended for relaxation during playtime. However, many French schools lack a specific room designated as a staffroom.

Organization of the schools

There is much variation in the size of the schools, ranging from the single-class village school to larger schools in towns, with up to 300 pupils. Large schools are more common in England than in France. As for the organization of the schools, it differs tremendously in the two countries.

Although on the whole both French and English primary schools cater for children between the ages of 6 and 11 (5–11 in England), there are five different levels in France, and seven in England, where class size is around 30 compared with around 25 in France. It is not unusual in England to find within the same class two different age levels, or even 'vertical groups'. In France, teachers often feel that classes made up of pupils with different levels are difficult to teach. In England, however, such classes are often the result of a conscious choice in terms of teaching technique.

In both countries the number of teachers appointed in any particular school depends on pupil numbers. Teaching posts in specific subject areas can be found when the need arises. In both countries, the current policy of integrating children with special educational needs (whether physical, mental or behavioural) within the normal school system means that a number of specialist posts exist (teachers for special needs, remedial teachers, psychologists). Educational psychologists, however, are much better integrated in the school system in France.

In France, schools located in 'priority zones' are allocated supplementary resources. The 1989 'loi d'orientation' introduced the notion that French teachers who work in schools located in those areas should be entitled to a supplementary allowance, equivalent to that formerly paid to English teachers in social priority areas, but there is much opposition to the actual payment of such an allowance both on the part of teachers and their unions, and on the part of parent associations.

The school day and the school year

The school year is organized in a very similar fashion in France and in England, with three terms separated by short Christmas and Easter holidays, and a 6–8-week summer break, with a week at half-term. The shorter school day in England is the reason for the shorter summer break (6 weeks).

For schoolchildren in England, the school day starts at around 9.00 a.m., and finishes at around 3.00 or 3.30 p.m. There is a break of 1 hour for lunch, which is normally taken at school; the children either bring their own packed lunch or use the school canteen. A minority of children go home for lunch. In England, children go to school 5 days a week, from Monday to Friday, and have a 25–27½ hour working week. In France, the working week for school children is 27 hours, compulsorily spread over nine half-days. Since there is no school on Wednesdays in order to allow children to attend religious instruction classes, all children go to school on Saturday morning. A number of very tentative attempts to end the practice of school on Saturdays, a practice which is part of the national directives, have invariably led to heated arguments, partly because of fears that the secular character of public schooling might be challenged in consequence.

What happens in class time in both countries is rather different. The fact remains, however, that on the whole the teaching to a greater or lesser extent revolves around the 'three Rs'.

In England, the children are engaged in various activities, either on their own or within a group, within the same class. Teachers sometimes organize their pupils' work for the whole week, so that all children have to take charge of their own work. For other children the work is organized on a daily basis, and activities alternate between groups. The teacher moves around the different groups as and when the need arises. The practice of teaching the whole class, which is a feature of French classrooms, is much rarer in England, and occurs only when new notions need to be presented, or with a view to getting the children to think about a specific question. Children work as individuals for a good part of the time, with some group and whole-class work. The emphasis in English schools is on the learning process more than on the acquisition of specific facts, and the various activities are selected in order to stimulate curiosity, to facilitate problem-solving, and to find solutions through experimentation. Work is often organized in a topic-based rather than a subject-based way. The topic-based approach may often include the three Rs.

In French classrooms, teaching to the whole class at once is still a fundamental practice, particularly for the three Rs, which tend to be taught in the morning; sports and the other curriculum subjects are taught in the afternoon, when teaching approaches can be more flexible, involving, for example, group work and children being able to move around the class. The detailed curriculum is no longer set by the national body as hitherto. Instead there are rather broad central directives. These directives specify the main objectives for each school year, and give a not inconsiderable amount of freedom to the teachers concerning both the area of teaching practice and of content. It seems, however, that as yet French teachers tend not to make use of this flexibility (Broadfoot and Osborn, 1987). This may be partly because there has been no systematic effort to set up provision for group planning and team-teaching among teachers. No provision is made, for instance, for discussion of work during school hours, and any teacher is at liberty to refuse to attend meetings which take place outside school hours. Moreover, the school head has no official role in this area. Training sessions do take place (as in England), where teachers can meet, and these no longer have to concentrate on topics chosen by the school inspector. But either these sessions are too few, or such matters are difficult to follow up, since they very rarely lead to any practical projects being organized.

The teachers

Teachers in France are State employees. Their status, rights, duties and responsibilities are all laid down in official texts. Teachers in England are employed by their local authority, and posts depend on the specific needs of schools. As a rule, they have a contract of employment. Unlike their French counterparts, they do not necessarily have tenure for life. The career of a French State employee is fundamentally stable in that the loss of a post does not lead to the post holder being unemployed, as he or she keeps both title and salary. It is up to the State to find him or her another post.

Training

In both countries, teacher training started in the nineteenth century, and the systems set up were closely linked to the historical development of the two school systems and the two societies concerned. In England, the Church of England had a leading role in the provision of teacher training. The objectives of the training were intricately connected to social and moral needs. In France, teacher training colleges (*écoles normales*) were set up along the lines of the German model. Although two different bodies were involved (the Catholic Church and the State), teacher training in France was fundamentally austere. The colleges were run along quasi-monastic lines, and adhered to a strict moral code, as well as being single-sex, in order to train teachers as models to be followed. This approach endured for many years. In England, the rationale informing teacher training was very similar. In both countries the moral code which prevailed in the nineteenth century was a fundamental influence in teacher training.

In both countries, a second path to becoming a teacher developed. In England, experienced teachers supervised new teachers with no teaching qualification on an apprenticeship model. In France, the recruitment of *brevet* holders (equivalent to GCSE or O level), and later of *baccalauréat* holders (equivalent to A level), was the method used to deal with increased demand when there was an inadequate supply of qualified teachers. However, unlike in England, those recruits were not supervised by their trained colleagues. This supervision was the responsibility of teaching advisers. Such differences in approach to a common problem reflect the fundamental difference between the two school systems. The French system promoted individualism within the school whereas the English system promoted teamwork. This is still very much a contrasting feature of the two school systems today.

In France, these two modes of training still apply, even though compulsory training at an *école normale* was instituted in 1981. The fact is, of course, that many practising teachers were recruited before 1981, and never went through a period of training (this was the case for 60 per cent of the teachers in the *département* of Bouches-du-Rhône in 1982 at the time of our study). Many changes have taken place in teacher training over the past twenty years following the institution of compulsory training for teachers in 1981. *Baccalauréat* holders took a 3-year course at an *école normale*. This course has undergone a number of modifications over the years. Teaching took place both at a university and at an *école normale*, and candidates had to pass the DEUG (*diplôme d'études universitaires générales*). Initially, the DEUG was specifically designed for teachers. They can now take any DEUG of their choice.

After 1986, prospective teachers had to have a DEUG (and not just the *baccalauréat*) before they could start teacher training, which is now done over 2 years.

The 1989 *loi d'orientation* raised entry requirements for teacher training to the Licence (bachelor's degree level) from 1992. Training became a one-year course at an *institut universitaire de formation des maîtres* (IUFM), done by university teachers, school inspectors, primary school teachers and others.

In England it has long been the expectation that all teachers in State primary schools will have received training. The training can take one of two major forms. Firstly there is the postgraduate route in which future teachers take a degree at university and then spend a year training to teach in primary schools, at the end of which they will be awarded a Post-Graduate Certificate in Education (PGCE). The alternative route is to gain a Bachelor of Education degree by studying at specialist training colleges, most of which have now become Colleges of Higher Education or have become incorporated into general higher educational institutions. The BEd qualification is now normally a four-year honours degree incorporating practical training and higher academic study at degree level. Thus, either way the new teacher entering the English primary classroom will now be likely to have spent 4 years studying either on the 3 plus 1 model or the 4 years' concurrent study and training approach. All students aspiring to teacher training must now possess five GCSEs, including Maths and English, and two A levels, the minimum requirement for higher education.

In the education of English primary teachers, there is considerable emphasis on art and craft, display work, creation of number games, integrated project work and so on, as well as the equally fundamental needs of any teacher in terms of controlling children and planning work which both matches the needs of the children and captures their interest. Those who are responsible for the education and training of future teachers include ex-teachers and advisers with long professional experience, and university teachers, who will provide the theoretical enrichment of the student's course.

Both countries have schemes for in-service training, although these are different. In France, such training is organized for each *département* by the *écoles normales*, the school inspectors and their teaching advisers. All practising teachers are entitled to a total in-service training of one whole school year spread over the whole teaching career, excluding the first and the last five years.

In England, in-service training can be either directly linked to primary school teaching, or involve taking a higher degree. There are also short courses organized in the schools or in teacher training colleges and departments. Such courses normally attempt to deal with specific teaching or school needs, which is not always the case in France.

The appointment system, and progress through the career ladder

One of the fundamental differences between the two countries is, as was mentioned earlier, that French teachers are tenured for life, whilst English teachers have individual contracts. Both are free to seek posts in other schools.

Teachers in England can apply for any job advertised. The criteria for specific appointments are defined by the local authority (LEA) or by the individual school. In most cases, a shortlist is drawn up and an interview follows with the appointment being made by the school governors, for whom this is a very important responsibility.

In France, a list of current and likely vacancies is drawn up for each *département* by the Inspection Académique. Teacher requests for new posts are assessed by means of a scheme which normally takes into account the number of years of experience of the individual teacher, the professional mark given to each teacher by the school inspector, and the family status, the exact system varying from one *département* to the next. The school head plays no part in the appointment procedure.

In England, it is common for primary school teachers to belong to one of the three teacher unions: the National Union of Teachers, AMMA or NASUWT. These unions led a sustained period of industrial action in the mid-1980s. Such action was a reflection both of teachers' unhappiness with the lack of funds available for education and of the perceived inadequacy of the pay rises offered. Eventually it was terminated by the Secretary of State for Education, who abolished the negotiating machinery through which bargaining between teachers' representatives and their employers, the local education authorities, had hitherto taken place and imposed a national settlement. Coupled with the scale of the demands now being made on teachers under the 1988 Education Reform Act, this has led to a good deal of unhappiness and stress among teachers at the present time (Osborn and Broadfoot, 1992b).

In France, after the initial bitter struggle of teachers, as civil servants, to be allowed to join trade unions was won in 1925, most elementary school teachers joined the

Syndicat National des Instituteurs (SNI). Until recently, the deep divide between the SNI and the Syndicat National des Enseignants Secondaires was reflected in very different status, pay and conditions at the two levels (Duclaud-Williams, 1980). Recently, however, the French government has introduced a common title, *professeur d'école*, and with it a common pay structure and conditions. Many ordinary classroom teachers complain that the SNI is too political, having relatively little concern with pedagogical issues and playing, instead, a major part at central government level in the process of policy-making.

In England, there has traditionally been nothing like the French system of inspection of teachers. The school head has been largely responsible for the behaviour and quality of the teaching staff, and her main function is, and has been, to manage a stable and efficient teaching team. Under local management of schools, governors are now responsible if there are any problems and in exceptional circumstances school governors can ask a specific teacher to resign if her performance does not fit in with the objectives of the school.

This cannot happen in France, where the school itself has no responsibility in this area. The French school head can provide guidance for inexperienced teachers, or give advice, but each teacher is in charge of a particular class that is her responsibility. The school inspector can only assess the performance of individual teachers. However, since school inspectors supervise a large number of schools, their visits to individual teachers are infrequent. Over the last few years, an effort has been made to ensure that each teacher is visited by the school inspector at least every other year. Some years ago, it was not unusual for teachers to see the school inspector only every few years. The outcomes of these visits are a report and a mark assessing the individual teacher's performance. These marks have an important function, since they are taken into account for appointments and promotion.

Although the 1988 Education Reform Act in England does not provide explicitly for inspection of individual teachers, the existence of national assessments, which will be aggregated by class and published at ages 7, 11, 14 and 16, suggests that consumers will be able to compare teachers on the basis of their pupils' results. This, plus the introduction of an 'appraisal' system for teachers suggests that the government is concerned to strengthen substantially traditional arrangements for 'quality control' of teachers in England.

The role of the school head

Both in France and in England, school heads are relieved of some of their teaching duties in order to deal with administrative tasks. The number of hours involved depends on the size of the school. In all but the smaller schools in England, headteachers are full-time in the post with no responsibility for a class or for regular teaching duties. The responsibilities of school heads are wide-ranging, from the smooth running of the school to relations with parents, local authorities and so on. And although in a sense the duties of school heads appear very similar in both countries, there is also a fundamental difference in what is expected of them. Recent attempts in France to give school heads more responsibility have led to strong opposition on the part of teachers; the school head must remain 'a teacher responsible for managing the school', and must not, as the ministry would have it, be placed in an elevated position.

In England, the teachers recognize that the school head has a fundamental leadership role to play in influencing the way teaching is done at their school, and all teachers feel a large degree of responsibility towards the head. The position is not seen as in any way usurping or threatening, and is seen as being essential to the co-ordinated delivery of the curriculum. Such a role for the school head is totally out of the question in France at the present time, because the teachers have a deeply ingrained sense of equality which means that they cannot accept the notion of one person being in a position superior to that of every other teacher in the school. Although the need is felt in France to get the teachers together in teams which could work on specific projects, both teachers and their unions feel that this can be achieved without a re-definition of the headteacher's role in the direction of extra power, provided that the State ensures that such teams can actually meet and work (by giving remission on teaching commitments, or by paying appropriate allowances).

Governors

In England, the headteacher is answerable in the first instance to the governing body of the school, which comprises representatives of teachers, parents, members of the local community and representatives of the local authority. Since the Education Act of 1980 made new statutory provision for elected teacher and parent governors, successive legislation has strengthened the power of governors to the point where, under the 1988 Education Reform Act, they are the body corporately responsible for every aspect of the school's educational and financial conduct. Predictably, the lack of a tradition of local school autonomy and the employment of teachers in France directly by the State has inhibited the evolution of anything equivalent to an English governing body. Although parents now form part of the *conseil d'école*, this body has little real power and certainly cannot interfere in decisions concerning employment of teachers or curriculum content.

Parents

In England, the substantially increased power of governors reflects in part a corre-sponding increase in the power of parents in recent years. Since 1980, not only have parents had a significantly greater role on school governing bodies, they have also had the right to express a preference for the school they would like their child to attend and, in theory, to have that preference complied with unless there are particular reasons why this request cannot be met.

At a less formal level, parents are actively involved in most primary schools. The focus for such involvement is often a parent–teacher association, which runs a variety of activities designed either to raise money for the school or to strengthen the partner-ship between teachers and parents in the educational enterprise. In most primary schools, parents have ready access to their child's teacher and classroom, and may be involved in a variety of support roles in the classroom or playground, or in extracur-ricular activities. Many primary schools are now actively seeking to enlist the help of parents to support their children at home in activities such as mathematics and reading.

As reported in subsequent chapters, French parents are much less likely to be seen as partners in the educational process by teachers, who guard jealously their professional territory from interference. This may include actual physical limits on how far parents come into the school premises. The parents' role is rather seen as involving the responsibility of caring for their child so that he arrives at school well-behaved and eager to receive what the teacher has to give.

OVERVIEW

At the time of this study, the English primary school was widely seen as a testimony to educational innovation. During the 1960s and 1970s there was a steady transformation of the traditional knowledge-based curriculum and formal teaching into a learning environment emphasizing discovery and experiment, enriched by a whole variety of objects and artefacts which can serve to encourage pupil learning. This change was largely achieved by the freedom schools and teachers enjoyed to develop educational practices in accord with their own professional ideologies. The very broadly based conception of the teacher's role, which, as subsequent chapters describe, causes so much heartache for English teachers, lies at the core of this professional ideology and is a long-standing feature of English primary school teaching.

The French primary school is, by contrast, a remarkable testimony to educational conservatism. Most classrooms are still characterized by an emphasis on the 'three Rs' and formal teaching. Although considerable freedom theoretically exists for teachers to experiment with new ideas and new teaching approaches, little use is made of this in practice. Most primary teachers still hold fast to the desirability of traditional practices and are uneasy with less orthodox approaches. The lack of any distinctive school identity and ethos and of a policy development role for the headteacher makes it difficult for teachers to envisage working collectively to support each other and for the school to respond to the specific characteristics of its clientele.

In England, by contrast, many primary teachers are feeling increasingly embattled at the present time – as a result of the effects of cuts in educational funding; by a decline in public confidence in educational outcomes; by pressures to return to a more utilitarian curriculum; and by the need to cope with a host of initiatives impacting on schools. However, they do have the support of colleagues and daily contact with fellow professionals, which often results in collaborative approaches to curriculum planning and teaching. The autonomy which has so long characterized the classroom and the school as a whole in England and which has led to teachers evolving a very broad conception of their role through their freedom to respond to their conceptions of pupil needs has also allowed the structures to evolve which are necessary to support this demanding professional commitment.

This chapter has set out briefly the characteristics of primary education in England and France at the time of the study. In England it is already clear that the changes currently being implemented will either serve to increase the existing emphasis on an individualized pedagogy by providing a more systematic structure against which to plan for the needs of each individual pupil, or by contrast they will stifle the creativity which currently characterizes primary school classrooms and lead to a return to teaching with externally determined objectives and competitive testing. In France the outcome of current changes may be a more collaborative and creative approach to classroom teaching. It may also be that the current challenge to deeply held convictions concerning the role of the head and the nature of the school will result in a major loss of morale and of the clear sense of direction which has hitherto characterized French primary teachers, as we shall see in the pages that follow. The evidence we present here can inform such speculation and thus provide a surer basis for future policy-making.

Chapter 4

The Design of the Study

Comparative studies between countries present problems, both in relation to the design of the research instruments and to the selection of the cohorts to be studied. These cannot be solved in a totally satisfactory way. The decisions which had to be made therefore required a very close collaborative effort, involving frequent meetings between the French and the English teams.

We discuss some of the problems which occurred as a result of the comparative nature of the study in the concluding sections of this chapter. First, however, we describe how the cohorts were selected within the chosen areas, before going on to consider the main research instrument, namely the questionnaire, and the way it was used.

POPULATIONS AND COHORTS

The research design involved a three-level strategy of questionnaire, interview and classroom observation. In addition, teachers were asked to keep diaries of their professional activities outside school hours. In this book we concentrate mainly on the questionnaire study, although some findings are presented from the classroom study and from more intensive interviews with teachers, in particular in Chapters 6 and 7. The first stage of the enquiry, the questionnaire survey, was based on two matched samples of 360 teachers in each country. The advantages of geographical proximity, as well as relative similarity, led to the decision to take the county of Avon as the basis for the English sample and the *département* of Bouches-du-Rhône for the French. In Avon the two major towns of Bristol and Bath match in many respects the conurbations of Marseilles and Aix-en-Provence, respectively. Bristol and Marseilles are large industrial ports with a rapidly growing tertiary sector; Bath and Aix are both historic spa towns with a heavy emphasis on tourism and the arts as well as some new developments and industry.

It was further decided to strengthen the comparative rigour, as well as deepening the potential interest of the enquiry, by drawing the sample from schools in four matched socio-economic zones – 'rural', 'inner-city', 'average working-class' and 'affluent middle-class'. This subdivision into zones provided for comparison intra-nationally as well as internationally. The two main criteria for this zone identification were the socio-economic status of the population and an index of 'social stress' based on levels of unemployment, number of immigrants, quality of housing and relative density as set out in statistics provided by the Institut National de la Statistique et des Études Économiques (1978) in France and Avon Planning Office (1981). Schools were chosen where the catchment areas most nearly conformed to the zone characteristics identified, and were selected on a stratified random basis with approximately 90 teachers in each zone.

The four clearly defined zones were as follows:

- *a rural zone*: often relatively prosperous, with some agriculture, although many inhabitants in both countries were commuters to the centres. Many of the rural schools were small with one form entry.
- *three urban zones*:
  - traditional, settled working-class areas where the accommodation might be either small houses or bungalows (common in England), or blocks of flats;
  - older inner-city areas with a sizeable proportion of ethnic minority population and a relatively high level of unemployment;
  - middle-class areas in the suburbs, with either privately owned houses or more luxurious blocks of flats, and a high proportion of professional and managerial families.

In the ensuing text, the four socio-economic zones* are described as follows:

Zone 1 – Rural (R)
Zone 2 – Traditional working-class (W)
Zone 3 – Inner-city areas (IC)
Zone 4 – Middle-class areas (M)

The classroom study sample

In addition to the major questionnaire survey, a programme of in-depth interviews and classroom observation was conducted with a sub-sample of teachers in each region in each country. This mixture of quantitative and qualitative methodologies was designed to enable us both to map the scale of difference in the perspective of teachers in the two countries, and to begin to understand some of the origins of these differences.

Sixteen teachers in each country were 'shadowed' for up to a week at a time and observed using a combination of field notes and a more systematic, but highly detailed, observation schedule adapted from Powell (1985). Each teacher was also interviewed and asked to keep a diary of her professional activities out of school hours for that week.

---

*The zones selected were as similar as possible in the two countries. However, in the inner-city zones selected in both countries, there were certain differences connected to the historical development of the two cities. The immigrant populations of the two countries are not identical. France has always had a particular interest in Africa and South-East Asia, and England in Asia. Even though in both cities the ethnic minority populations concerned are rather badly tolerated, and suffer from a lack of opportunities, their history and culture are quite different. For example, in France many are first-generation immigrants, whilst this is not the case in England. Finally, in the inner-city zone, all French schools have a higher proportion of ethnic minority children than is the case in English schools. The fact remains however that those two zones are very similar if we consider the economic and social difficulties of the people living there.

The 16 teachers selected for detailed study were chosen from one or more of what were identified as 'ideal-type' schools in each of the four socio-economic zones.

THE QUESTIONNAIRE

Preparation of the questionnaire

Several options were possible in order to elicit information from the teachers regarding their own conceptions of their work and their professional responsibilities. We chose the questionnaire with direct questions (see Selltiz *et al.*, 1965; Cohen and Manion, 1987) with a large number of fixed-response items. This meant that the aim of the questionnaire was made clear to the teachers, particularly since an explanatory letter was included. This decision was taken because of the ease with which non-open-ended questions can be analysed by computer, and the relative objectivity of the comparisons established. In addition, several open-ended questions about teachers' work and responsibility were included, enabling teachers to respond at some length in their own words. Finally, after the questionnaire data had been collected and preliminary analysis had been carried out, in-depth interview and classroom observation were carried out with a sub-sample of the initial cohort. The results of these more qualitative data are largely published elsewhere (although some are presented in Chapter 6), but they and the replies to the open-ended questions do confirm the broad findings of the questionnaire study in most respects.

As well as dealing with the problems that particularly accompany studies involving the use of questionnaires, we had to take into account problems which were specific to our comparative approach. One of the major difficulties concerns linguistic problems arising from translation. We had to ensure that the words and expressions used in the two languages covered identical concepts.

The word *responsabilité* covers two concepts, one philosophical, with liberty as its corollary, the other political, with notions of law and obligation as its corollary. In English the two senses are clearly defined through the use of two different words, 'responsibility' and 'accountability'. This is not the case in French, where only one word exists, *responsabilité*.

Also, for a number of words a paraphrase had to be used rather than a single word, in order to retain the underlying meaning. It was not always possible to solve these translation problems satisfactorily, and so some compromises had to be reached in order to collect comparable data.

Before the questionnaire in its present form was finalized, a number of pilot versions were used with some 50 teachers, both English and French. Both the results and the teachers' comments were taken into account for the preparation of the final version of the questions and the suggested answers.

Format of the questionnaire

The questionnaire consisted of 34 questions (see Appendix 1) which fell into two main groups, the first group comprising factual questions and the second group asking for opinions. The analysis of the replies to these 34 questions forms the organizing principle for Parts II and III of this book. The replies to the factual questions allowed us to draw up a personal and professional profile of the teachers (Part II). The replies to the questions eliciting teachers' opinions gave us information on what the teachers said about their job, their function and the way they practised their job (Part III).

The factual questions which form Part II of the book ('Teachers and Their Working Environment')

These cover three different areas:

- personal and professional information about the teachers themselves (questions 7 to 10 and 18 to 34);
- the socio-demographic description of the place of work: schools, classes (questions 1 to 7);
- contracts and exchanges between teachers and with para-educational staff (questions 11 to 14).

As well as enabling us to form a picture of the characteristics of the 'typical' French and 'typical' English primary teacher, these questions make it possible to examine the extent to which the personal characteristics of the individual teacher may interact with variables at institutional and national level in influencing teacher ideologies and practices.

The questions eliciting opinions

The most important part of the questionnaire is that concerned with the teachers' perception of the nature of their work and their responsibilities.

These questions form four dimensions which will dictate the organization of the first four chapters in Part III:

- general perceptions of the nature of the teacher's job;
- professional responsibility and objectives;
- influences, constraints and degree of freedom in teachers' work;
- accountability.

These questions have two different formats. Some involve the teacher selecting one of several fixed responses; the rest are open-ended questions which leave the teacher completely free to express her opinions. Twelve questions attempt to find out what teachers think of their work, and in that group question 18, an open-ended question ('What does "professional responsibility" mean for you as a teacher?'), is the most important. The answers to that question allowed us to explore aspects which had not been dealt with in the fixed-response questions, and also brought complementary information to the replies given to those questions. The results of the analysis of that central question will be integrated within all of the chapters which deal with the four themes selected.

Questions dealing with general perceptions of teaching as a job

This concerns mostly question 27, and also parts of the answers to question 18.

Questions dealing with the teachers' objectives

Questions 21 and 22 deal with the goals of teaching, in other words with the objectives which the teachers hold in relation to their practice. Question 21 lists 19 objectives (see Appendix 1 for a detailed list), from academic learning itself to more general educational objectives. Question 22 (a semi-open-ended question) deals with the long-term responsibility that teachers feel they have regarding the overall education of the children. The replies to question 18 cover mostly the perceptions that the teachers have of the nature of their work, and the place of the objectives to be reached.

Questions dealing with constraints, influences and freedom in professional practice

Questions 15, 16, 17 and 20, together with a number of items of question 25, attempt in a very general way to elicit opinions on the influences and constraints which apply in the practice of the teacher's job. Question 17, and items 1–3, 5, 7–10, 13 and 16 of question 25, give us information on the relative importance of some factors which might influence teachers. Questions 19 and 20, and items 12 and 15 of question 25, deal with the amount of freedom and the constraints experienced in relation to the content and the methods of teaching. Finally, questions 15 and 16 deal with the various influences which can exercise control on the teacher's job.

Questions dealing with accountability

Question 23 deals with the notion of accountability. It attempts to establish whether teachers feel accountable in terms of the classroom, or whether they do so within a much wider educational context. Although the replies to statements 4, 6, 11, 14 and 17 of question 25 add more detail on this topic, it is particularly the replies to question 18 which give complementary information on the aspects covered by question 23.

COLLECTION AND ANALYSIS OF THE DATA

Collection of the data

The study was carried out with the full support of the local authorities and the schools. The heads of schools were notified of our visit by their authority, and in England permission was also sought from the heads individually. This was necessary because of the differences in the two systems described in Chapter 2. The heads were invariably very helpful.

The researchers took the questionnaires to the schools, and picked them up a few days later, after the teachers had had enough time to complete them. Every attempt was made to respect the anonymity of the individual teachers, who had the option of returning the completed questionnaires in sealed unmarked envelopes. Completing the questionnaires took less than one hour. The response rate after follow-ups was 68 per cent in France and 75 per cent in England, although there were variations in this respect within each country, depending on the location of the schools. In France, in rural areas, where the schools are smaller, the response rate was always better (96 per cent). This is perhaps because contact between researcher and teacher was closer than in urban areas. This variation can also be explained by the fact that in Marseilles the teachers from urban schools are more frequently asked to help with various studies, this being the case particularly in inner-city areas with a large immigrant population (56 per cent response rate), where schools are under considerable pressure from outside (social workers, the press, other researchers, etc.).

In England, where the response rate was invariably slightly better, the location of the schools did not play such an important role. It is worth noting, however, that the rate of response was slightly less good in inner-city areas (65 per cent), probably for the same reasons as in France.

Analysis of the data

The data collected were analysed by computer at the University of Bristol and at the Centre de Recherche en Psychologie de l'Éducation at the University of Aix-en-Provence using two separate data sets which were then merged.

The analysis of the fixed-response questions was done with the traditional tools of descriptive statistics: frequency distribution, cross-tabulation, etc. Subsequent analysis included principal-components analysis.

In analysing the responses to the open-ended questions, a procedure involving the analysis of themes similar to that described by Woods (1986) and by Burgess (1984) was adopted, but with the added cross-cultural dimension making it essential for the French and English researchers to work together in sifting and sorting the data and identifying the issues. Particular care had to be given to choosing categories which would have the same degree of relevance for the analysis of replies from both countries. The first step was to establish the major categories emerging from the responses and to identify the sub-groups within each category. Whilst it was relatively easy for the English researchers to identify categories relevant to the English data, a more attenuated process was involved in establishing general categories relevant to both, and this involved both teams in sorting and sifting the data, refining and clarifying the initial categories established at each further stage of the process. More generally, throughout the study great care was taken that the teams in the two countries worked closely together during the design and analysis stages. Such close contact is an essential component of comparative research of this type and without it we would have been unable to resolve many of the difficulties which arose.

PROBLEMS OF CROSS-CULTURAL RESEARCH

Earlier sections of this chapter have touched upon some of the difficulties which have to be resolved in a cross-cultural research project of this nature. These include:

1. conceptual equivalence;
2. equivalence of measurement;
3. linguistic equivalence;
4. sampling.

Although these problems may arise with any research method, they are brought into sharpest form by the questionnaire/survey method as used in the 'Bristaix' study (Warwick and Osherson, 1973).

Conceptual equivalence

One of the most basic theoretical questions in comparative analysis is whether the concepts which are being researched have any equivalent meaning in the cultures under study. Concepts may be more or less culturally specific – even, as emerged from this study, such an apparently unambiguous one as 'teaching style'.

Particular terms may not have exact counterparts in all cultures. A major challenge for comparative research then is to provide conceptual definitions that have equivalent, though not necessarily identical meaning, in various cultures. These problems are lessened to some extent, but not eliminated, when comparing two Western industrialized societies. There may be more shared concepts, but there are still problems of conceptual equivalence. For example, in the Bristaix study 'accountability' has no equivalent meaning in French and therefore the expression 'professional responsibility' was chosen, since it appeared to have validity in both countries.

Equivalence of measurement

In addition to choosing variables that can be given comparable conceptual definitions in the societies under study, there is the further challenge of developing equivalent indicators for the concepts. Concepts may differ in their salience for the culture as a whole, or respondents in some countries may be unwilling to discuss sensitive topics such as politics, sexual behaviour, income or religion. For example, Lerner (1956) notes that it is impossible 'to make discreet enquiries about religion among the French'. Finally, the salience of a concept may vary because respondents are unable or unused to discussing it.

A similar problem occurred in the Bristaix study, where French teachers were not able to describe their 'teaching style'. A possible explanation for this may well be that this was not seen as a problematic issue in France, and that French teachers were not accustomed to reflect upon their 'teaching style' in an analytical way.

Dujykes and Rokkhan (1954) have suggested that one effective approach to equivalence lies in a study design involving collaboration between researchers in participating societies. They indicate a number of ways in which this may be achieved, but conclude that by far the most direct approach to equivalence is the 'joint-development-concurrent' model, where the research design is arrived at jointly by collaborators from the different cultures involved and the study is carried out more or less simultaneously in these cultures. This is the approach adopted in the Bristaix study, which allowed at least some of these important methodological difficulties to be overcome.

Linguistic equivalence

There still remains the difficulty of obtaining linguistic equivalence through translation. 'Back-translation' was seen for a time as the answer to these difficulties, in which the questionnaire is translated from language A to language B by a native speaker of B, then from B to A by a native speaker of A, then from A to B by a third party, and so on until discrepancies in meaning are clarified or removed. This approach has recently come under heavy fire, however, since it does not guarantee conceptual equivalence.

Warwick and Osherson (1973) offer some suggestions as a guide to setting the problem of linguistic equivalence within the broader framework of conceptualization and research design. These include ensuring that the research problem is salient to all the cultures involved; that the primary emphasis in translation is on the conceptual equivalence – comparability of ideas – rather than of words *per se*; and that there is extensive pre-testing of the research instruments in the local culture.

The Bristaix study attempted to confront these problems by employing a method emphasizing joint production of research instruments by the researchers from both countries in the process of which concepts and their meanings could be extensively discussed.

Sampling problems

The comparability of cross-societal studies may be greatly reduced by, for example, the use of non-comparable or low-quality sampling frames; differing procedures for setting the sample; the oversampling of some groups and undersampling of others; high, or varying, non-response rates. The Bristaix project attempted to overcome these dangers by using a method of quota sampling that attempted to ensure comparability of the sample. Non-response was minimized as much as possible by personal collection of questionnaires from every school in the sample in France and by telephone call and personal collection from all schools which did not respond to the first follow-up letter in England.

Finally, Warwick and Osherson make the point that many of the problems previously discussed stem from an exclusive reliance on single methodologies. They make a plea for more 'innovative combinations of methods in comparative research'. Many of the limitations of survey methods in comparative study, for example, would be much less serious 'if the study also contained extensive qualitative information on the societies covered'. The combination of survey and ethnographic methods in comparative research is a fruitful one and provides the analyst with additional sources of information for interpreting the findings, as well as immediate evidence on the validity of the data. The Bristaix study is one of relatively few comparative studies that have attempted to combine methods in this way.

Another strong case for including an ethnographic stage in survey design is made by Crossley and Vulliamy (1984), who have suggested that case study or ethnographic methods can play a vital role in comparative education in examining the hiatus that may exist between the policies and the practice of schooling. Case studies of schooling can expose the gap between rhetoric and reality and lead to theories about the processes of schooling. They can also, in combination with questionnaire surveys, act as a method of 'triangulation', helping to atone for some of the problems inherent in the questionnaire/survey method. For example, it is well known that questionnaire surveys alone are prone to 'the reproduction of rhetoric'; that respondents are often unwilling to admit 'failures' or doubts about what they are doing; and that there is a tendency for respondents to present what they think researchers want to hear. In addition, surveys tend to make assumptions about the meaning of both concepts and actions for the respondents and, in the positivist tradition, necessarily tend to impose the researcher's meaning on the respondents. As cited previously, these problems can be intensified in cross-cultural research.

There is thus a strong case for combining qualitative and quantitative approaches in cross-national comparisons, and this is what the Bristaix study has sought to do in its three-level strategy including questionnaire, interview and classroom observation. Perhaps the most important area to get right in cross-cultural research, however, is that of working collaboratively with researchers in the countries under study. As described earlier, at all stages of the research process, but particularly during the design of the research instruments and the coding and analysis of the data, frequent contact was maintained between the French and English researchers through meetings lasting several days as well as by telephone and postal contact. This was vital in enabling the research team to reduce the problems outlined above, and to arrive at shared meanings and interpretations of the data.

Part II

The Teachers and Their Working Environment

The data presented in Part II of the book relate to the part of our study which attempted to elicit information on the teachers themselves (who are they?), their working environment (schools, classes and pupils) and their professional relationship with other people.

Although the data collected cover only a limited number of selected aspects, it will be apparent that a number of important differences emerged between the two countries. An awareness of those differences is useful for two reasons. First of all, we have to ask why it is that in two countries which are so close geographically, the educational system, although it shares many common characteristics, also demonstrates huge differences in a number of socio-demographic characteristics. Those differences themselves become the possible source of variations. In particular, we shall consider the way in which these differences contribute to a better understanding of teachers' ideologies as reported in Part III and how they shed light upon the nature of teaching and the influences upon it.

Chapter 5

Personal and Professional Profiles

In this chapter we examine the characteristics of the teachers in this study: their age, gender, position in school, qualifications and professional experience, and their professional relations with colleagues and other adults involved in the educational process. We conclude by constructing an 'identikit' profile of a typical French and a typical English teacher. The similarities and differences between the cohorts in the two countries shed light on a number of conceptual differences in the running of the two educational systems and have important implications for the differing conceptions of professional responsibility held by the two cohorts of teachers, which we explore in Part III of the book.

PERSONAL CHARACTERISTICS AND PROFESSIONAL TRAINING

An analysis of the personal and professional profiles of the teachers shows that in both the French and the English cohorts the profession of primary school teacher is dominated by women. The feminization of the teaching profession in all Western countries is a well-known phenomenon. The respective figures for both cohorts are very similar (68 per cent of the French teachers and 60 per cent of the English are women). On the whole, also, there is little difference between the ages of the teachers from both cohorts. The majority are aged from 31 to 45 (48 per cent of French and 57 per cent of English teachers), with about one-third aged over 45 in both cohorts. But these general similarities do not prevent the existence of marked differences which can be attributed to fundamental differences in the conception and running of the two educational systems.

Education and training

There is a significant difference in the length of training received by teachers in the two countries and in the importance of a university course within that training. At the time of the study, English teachers joined the profession after a longer period of training, and more of them had followed a course of study at university. Among the

English teachers, 81 per cent had a Certificate in Education, obtained after a post-A-level course of studies at a college of education. This was a non-university training course lasting 3 years. It no longer exists as an option, and all teachers entering primary education now have a degree. Among those teachers, 8 per cent had gone on to get further qualifications, and had a diploma in Advanced Studies, obtained after 1 year of full-time study (or 2 years' half-time) of a university-level course. Another mode of entry into the profession is to study for a 3-year university Bachelor of Education degree. Fifteen per cent of the English teachers in the cohort had a BEd, and 20 per cent had a degree of some sort. For those having university degrees other than a BEd, training then involves a 1-year PGCE course (12 per cent of the cohort). Three per cent of the cohort had the qualification of MEd (Master of Education).

In France, nearly all of the teachers (98 per cent) had the CAP (*certificat d'aptitude pédagogique*), obtained after 2 years, and for many of them after only 1 year* of a teacher-training course, done at an *école normale*. This course (with the exception of the few very young teachers in our cohort) is not of university standard, and is taken by *baccalauréat* holders after secondary school. Only one teacher in ten had a university diploma, the majority of these being young teachers. The setting of the new regulations regarding the training of primary school teachers in France should help to reduce this imbalance in so far as the 2-year training period in an *école normale* will now have to take place after a 2-year course of study at university, in any subject, leading to the DEUG. The creation of university courses in the area of education should also enable those French primary school teachers who wish to improve their qualifications to do so, and thereby to reduce those differences with the English system.

A second difference concerns teachers' position in the school. Our data reflect the fact that in French primary schools there are only two positions, head and teacher, whilst the English primary school system has a more definite career structure in which a classroom teacher can take on posts with special responsibility and has the possibility of becoming a deputy head and eventually a headteacher by moving schools and seeking promotion.

At this point, it is useful to repeat what was said on this subject in Chapter 2, namely that the French primary school system, a very centralized and hierarchical system at the national level, runs schools within which there is little hierarchy. The heads have essentially administrative duties and, at the time of the study, did not interfere with the teaching duties of their colleagues. At the time of the study, the English primary school system, a very decentralized system at the national level, with less hierarchy, had schools within which there was considerably more variety regarding areas of responsibility within the curriculum, and considerably more hierarchy.

Teaching experience

Despite the small differences regarding age, the teachers from the French cohort had been teaching and in their current posts for considerably longer than the teachers from the English cohort. The average figures for our two cohorts were 49 per cent of the French teachers with more than 20 years' teaching experience, as opposed to only 27 per cent of the English cohort; on the other hand, 24 per cent of the English

---

*The period of training for primary school teachers was increased to 2 years in France relatively recently. The older teachers therefore trained for only 1 year.

Table 5.1   *Gender and age of teachers in inner-city and affluent middle-class schools*

Population	Age	Zone 3: Inner city			Zone 4: Middle-class		
		M (%)	F (%)	Total (%)	M (%)	F (%)	Total (%)
French	<30 yrs	23.7	14.7	38.4	–	–	–
	31–45 yrs	18.5	29.5	48.0	6.7	27.0	33.7
	>45 yrs	6.2	7.4	13.6	11.3	55.0	66.3
		100		100	100		100
English	<30 yrs	2.2	4.6	6.8	6.7	5.6	12.3
	30–45 yrs	22.8	39.7	62.5	30.3	25.9	56.2
	>45 yrs	14.8	15.9	30.7	7.9	23.6	31.5
		100		100	100		100

teachers and 19 per cent of the French teachers had less than 10 years' teaching experience. One explanation for this difference is the longer training period, but probably the main reason is that higher proportions of English women leave teaching to have a family and then return after a period of absence. French women teachers are more likely to stay in post during early child-rearing.

When it comes to length of time in their current post, 63 per cent of French teachers and 53 per cent of English teachers had been teaching in their present schools for 6 years or more. This reflects the fact that in England it is thought necessary to change schools to advance in the career structure, whilst in France there is little conception of a career structure for primary teachers.

The influence of the location of the school

However, far more striking differences emerge between the two cohorts when we compare teachers working in schools in different areas. The location of the schools in our four different socio-economic zones had very different consequences for our two cohorts. In France the location of the school led to important differences, those differences being particularly spectacular at the two extremes of our range – the middle-class zone and the inner city; no such differences were recorded for the English cohort. For example, in the French middle-class zones, more than one teacher in every two (55 per cent) was a women over the age of 45, whilst this was the case for only one teacher in every four (24 per cent) in England. In the inner-city zone, there were ten times as many young men in the French cohort as there were in the English cohort: one French teacher in every four (24 per cent) was a man under 30, compared to only two teachers in 100 in England (Table 5.1).

Similarly, when we examined the teaching experience of teachers working in different socio-economic areas, striking differences emerged among the French cohort while there was little variation from zone to zone in the English cohort. To summarize, it was in the French inner-city areas where the least experienced teachers were to be found in the highest numbers, while those with the longest teaching experience had migrated to schools in affluent areas (Table 5.2).

Tallying with the age differences mentioned above, at least four teachers in every ten in the French inner-city zones had less than 10 years' teaching experience, whilst this

Table 5.2   *Years of experience in teaching of teachers in inner-city and affluent middle-class schools*

Population	Experience	Percentage of teachers		
		Zone 3: Inner city	Zone 4: Middle-class	T Mean* (%)
French (n = 360)	<5 yrs	12.5	–	6.9
	5–10 yrs	29.2	2.1	12.5
	11–20 yrs	37.5	18.5	31.7
	>20 yrs	20.8	79.4	48.9
		100	100	100
English (n = 360)	<5 yrs	5.7	6.7	6.0
	5–10 yrs	21.6	12.4	17.9
	11–20 yrs	50.0	58.4	48.8
	>20 yrs	22.7	22.5	27.4
		100	100	100

*For teachers in all four zones.

was the case for only 2 teachers in 100 in the middle-class zone. Conversely, there were around four teachers in every five (79 per cent) in the French middle-class zones, and only one teacher in every five (21 per cent) in the inner city (i.e. four times less), who had more than 20 years' teaching experience. This phenomenon reached nothing like the same proportions in the English cohort, whatever the zone. In the inner city, there was the same proportion of more experienced teachers as there was in the middle-class zone: 23 per cent in both cases. As for the younger teachers (less than 10 years' teaching experience), although there was a trend similar to the French one, the difference was considerably less marked (27 per cent as opposed to 19 per cent). For the English cohort, it was in the rural zone that the proportion of more experienced teachers was the highest, but the figures (36 per cent) were nowhere near as high as in the French middle-class zone. In other words, the observations relating to the number of years of teaching experience tallied entirely with those relating to the age of the teachers: in the English cohort, there were no differences between each zone which would correspond to differences in the degree of appeal of each particular zone, whilst for the French cohort there were spectacular differences, and these mostly between the inner city and the most affluent areas.

These important demographic differences can be explained by different career patterns and by the different system in use for the appointment of teachers in the two countries. The centralized system for educational appointments and transfers which applies to the French primary school teacher is based on a scale which gives age a priority rating. This system, which the professional bodies are very keen to preserve, leads to a situation which is quite different from the English system, where appointments are made by local education authorities to individual schools, and where the head and governors of a particular school are involved in the appointment. It therefore follows that a teacher's career progresses in different ways in England and in France.

For English teachers, age, sex and the number of years at the current school have little effect on appointments from one zone to the next. The fact that the teacher is a man or a woman, or has been in the profession for a shorter or a longer period of time, does not affect his or her chances of getting a post in a particular type of area.

In France, inexperienced teachers simply do not stand a chance of teaching in the affluent middle-class schools (which are seen by them as the most attractive). Posts in those areas are a privilege for older teachers, more particularly women. Conversely, the younger and less experienced teachers tend to be posted to the less privileged areas, regardless of the fact that children and families in those areas may need experienced teachers whose teaching skills have been refined to the maximum of their ability. This is no small paradox for an educational system which, whilst developing a well-known humanistic ideology in favour of the disadvantaged, perpetuates an appointment system which allocates the less experienced teachers to those same disadvantaged groups!

SOCIAL AND PROFESSIONAL RELATIONS

A common remark about primary school teachers is that theirs is a lonely job. The stereotype referred to here is that of adults locked up all day within the four walls of a classroom, isolated in their work, and sole determiners of the destinies of the pupils for whom they are responsible. Although the teacher's function is fundamentally a social one, this common perception of the teacher's role suggests a function exercised in total isolation from the rest of society. To what extent is this a caricature, and is there some truth in this view of things? Are primary school teachers really so isolated? Do they not in fact have a close working relationship with many other adults who also have an interest, to a greater or lesser extent and for various reasons, in the education of the pupils in their charge, for example parents, colleagues and other professionals? Does the primary school teacher's universe consist exclusively of school and classroom? Is it focused on classroom activities only? Or is it a wider professional universe, which would include other socio-educational activities? In other words, what do the working lives of our 720 French and English teachers look like? Do they approximate more closely to the stereotype of the isolated worker whose educational horizons are restricted on the whole to the classroom, or to team workers, collaborative professionals, who belong to a wider socio-educational universe with boundaries beyond the school proper?

Relationships with colleagues

Teachers were asked to specify how often they worked in close collaboration with colleagues when teaching their class or another group of pupils. It is striking that more than a third (38 per cent) of the French teachers from our cohort said that they never share their teaching responsibilities, whilst this was the case for only one English teacher in eight (12 per cent).

Conversely, more than one English teacher in two (58 per cent) said that such sharing took place more than once a week, and in fact one in four (25 per cent) said that this happened every day, or very nearly, whilst the corresponding figures for the French cohort were around half these proportions (30 per cent and 14 per cent). This difference in the sharing of teaching responsibilities appears in all socio-economic zones; it is most marked in the rural areas and least marked in the inner city. The particular practice mentioned most often (roughly 50 per cent of cases for both cohorts) is group work: a group of pupils from one class joins another group of pupils from another class, or from several other classes, for a common activity organized by the relevant teachers, and supervised by one of them. The normal classroom unit is broken up,

Table 5.3   *Frequency of collaboration with colleagues in teaching pupils*

Frequency of collaboration	Mean percentage	
	France	England
Never	37.9	12.4
Less than once a week	6.8	13.0
Once a week	25.1	16.5
More than once a week	16.7	32.7
Daily or almost daily	13.5	25.4
	100	100

and the pupils are redistributed according to different criteria: a common interest, similar levels, etc.

The much higher frequency of collaboration between colleagues which can be observed in English schools (Table 5.3) is linked to differences in the two educational systems. In the English system, the amount of freedom given to teachers in the selection of objectives and teaching methods, and the existence of teachers with specific responsibilities for certain subjects (see Chapter 2), led to a greater collaborative effort between teachers. And this feature was reinforced by the greater heterogeneity of levels within the same class, which led to the groups being made up of pupils from different classes for specific activities.

The influence of the location of the school

The lack of collaboration between teachers is in fact much more widespread in France than the average figures quoted above imply. It is in fact because of the teaching methods used in the inner city that the figure was low as 38 per cent. In the affluent middle-class zone the figure was almost 40 per cent, and in the rural zone and the average working-class zone it was somewhere between 45 and 50 per cent. The stereotype of the isolated worker is still therefore very much a reality in France, except for the inner city, where only one teacher in five replied that there is no collaboration at all, and four teachers in every ten (42 per cent) said that collaboration takes place more than once a week (22 per cent) or practically every day (21 per cent).

Again, in France the situation is very different in the inner city, whilst this is not so much the case in England. This can be explained easily. Firstly, the various measures adopted in schools located in disadvantaged areas (extra teaching posts, specialist or not, and an encouragement to practise group teaching) lead to groups of pupils being taken over by teachers other than the class teacher, with her collaboration. The second reason is that the difficulties associated with those schools, and the fact that teachers are often at a loss as to how to handle them, lead to their seeking effective help from other colleagues more often than in other zones. Difficulties lead to teamwork. Finally, this trend is probably reinforced by the fact that the teachers in the French inner city tend to be young teachers (see Chapter 4), whose recent training has probably made them more aware of teamwork than their older colleagues. It is interesting to note, by the way, that in a country where the traditional model of the isolated teacher is still very much alive, it is once again through steps (official or not) taken to deal with difficult pupils that teachers are forced to adopt different teaching methods.

Table 5.4 *Contact with parents: percentage of teachers responding in each category*

Type of contact	FRANCE				ENGLAND			
	1	2	3	4	1	2	3	4
Participating in activities in class	57.7	23.6	9.1	9.6	33.0	13.0	2.7	51.2
Discussing child's progress	2.0	35.0	35.0	28.0	1.2	60.7	19.4	18.7
Organizing social activities	31.1	53.7	8.8	6.4	25.7	56.2	13.7	4.2
At PTA meetings	17.7	68.7	9.8	3.8	34.5	47.0	17.7	0.7
By letter or telephone	35.2	30.2	19.6	15.0	8.3	43.5	21.1	27.1
Accompanying children on outings	17.9	64.1	11.8	6.2	9.4	78.9	7.9	3.8
Meeting by chance	21.6	28.5	15.1	34.8	2.7	20.7	18.0	58.7

Key:
1: Never
2: Less than once a month
3: At least once a month
4: At least once a week

For the English cohort, it is not in the inner city but in the rural areas that we found the largest number of teachers (70 per cent) who said they worked in collaboration with colleagues more than once a week, and the smallest number of teachers (7 per cent) who said that collaboration never took place. This can perhaps be explained by the fact that since rural schools are often small schools (see Chapter 4), many classes consist of children of very different age groups. This therefore leads to an even closer collaboration between colleagues than is the case elsewhere. Sometimes, for example, the numbers are such that a part-time teacher can be employed in addition to the class teacher, and this person may work with specific age groups for different activities during part of the week.

Relationships with parents

Table 5.4 shows that, on the whole, the teachers from our English cohort tended to have more contact with the parents of their pupils than their French counterparts. The differences recorded also vary according to the type and purpose of the contact involved. The difference is therefore not only quantitative but also qualitative.

This difference is two-fold: according to the teachers, contact with parents in England is less formal, and more often involves the parents in teaching activities. For instance, if we consider contacts that took place at least once a month, telephone calls or letters were involved for half (48 per cent) of the teachers, and chance meetings for three-quarters (76 per cent), whilst the corresponding figures for the French cohort were only respectively one-third (35 per cent) and half (50 per cent). Again, it was more common in England than in France (34 per cent compared with 18 per cent) that contact with parents should occur outside formal parent–teacher meetings. These figures lead to an impression of greater availability on the part of the English primary school teacher, since greater use is made of chance encounters to talk with parents.

It is also striking that almost seven English teachers in every ten (67 per cent) said that the parents of their pupils took part in classroom activities, half of them (51 per cent) even saying that this happened at least once a week. The situation is almost exactly the opposite in France. Almost six teachers in every ten (60 per cent) said that parents never took part in school activities, and when such participation did take place the frequency was low: only one teacher in every ten (10 per cent) said that this happened at least once a week. These differences in the amount of parental involvement inside the classroom have to be seen in the context of the regulations that apply. In France, these regulations are very restrictive: although permission is generally granted, non-school staff are not allowed on school premises without permission of the school inspector. Such a regulation does not make parental involvement easy, when there is a wish for it. But it is also true to say that many French teachers are still reluctant to let anyone into their classrooms who might be in a position to impinge on their power and their responsibilities.

However, the frequency of meetings with parents to discuss the child's progress is higher for the French cohort: such meetings were at the time of the study said to occur at least once a week for six French teachers in every ten (63 per cent), as opposed to four English teachers in every ten. Such meetings often take place if there is a particular problem, either at the family's request or at the teacher's request. The difference recorded in this area may mean that the French educational system with its norm-referenced objectives and its punishing pace leads to more children having problems (for example, it is common for children to have to repeat a year) than the English system; and/or that the French teacher, being more preoccupied with results, again because of the official programmes and the norm-referenced objectives, reacts more readily to the problems that occur. A meeting with parents to resolve a problem at school has sometimes resulted initially in alarming parents and pupils, even if it was set up because of a genuine wish to deal with the problem together in order to improve things. The eventual benefit derived from such a meeting naturally depends on the way these meetings take place, and on the interaction which results between family, school and pupil.

The influence of the location of the school

Whatever the type of contact (including parent–teacher meetings), and whatever the country, it is the teachers from the inner city who had the lowest frequency of contact with parents, and those from the rural and affluent middle-class areas who had the highest frequency of contact with parents. The relative difference, however, between the inner city and the other areas is greater in France than it is in England. For instance, the French teachers from the inner city were less than half as likely as the teachers from affluent middle-class areas (19 per cent compared with 43 per cent) to have contacts at least once a week through chance meetings, whilst for the English cohort the relative difference was much smaller, since the corresponding figures were 50 per cent and 64 per cent.

This may be partly a result of the reluctance of French inner-city parents, who may have negative feelings towards school deriving from their own childhood, to make contact with the teacher. It is also possible that, because of the difficult working conditions to be found in the inner-city zone, the teachers also have a tendency to expect little benefit for their pupils from contact with their parents. The task of ensuring that the parents feel involved in the school, that they feel at home there, that they are interested in its daily running and that there should be real collaboration between teachers and parents, is not an easy one. In France at the time of this study it did not appear to be encouraged in any way by the educational system.

Relations with other professionals

In both countries, and for all four zones, contact with para-educational staff tends to be not with social workers, who might be seen as attempting to ameliorate social and family conditions, but with remedial teachers, psychologists and others who work directly with the child, through a variety of techniques, with a view to correcting specific problems. The choice of these various professionals does not seem to be based on the same reasons for the two cohorts. For the English cohort, the help of those professionals was not sought any more often in the inner-city zone than in the other areas. The steps taken to seek help were more often in the area of academic work, because of the amount of freedom that the teachers had in the choice of the curriculum, and also because of the fairly flexible teaching methods.

The hierarchical nature of the French educational system seems to be responsible for the high frequency of referral to these various specialists in schools located in disadvantaged areas: on the one hand, because the smaller amount of autonomy granted to individual schools does not allow for the same flexibility in teaching practices; and on the other hand because, since the system includes remedial facilities within schools (the GAPP), the teachers make use of these facilities. The existence of these ameliorating services means that fundamental change in the system is less likely. It also contributes to or reflects a narrower and more restricted conception of the teacher's role.

SUMMARY

In this chapter we have emphasized some of the important similarities and differences which emerged in the personal and professional characteristics and working relationships of the French and English teachers in our study.

In a very striking way, and whatever the location of the school, the English primary school teacher, unlike her French counterpart, differs strongly from the stereotype of the isolated worker which is still very much alive in the popular imagination as being typical of the profession. In England, as we have seen, teachers have more contact with parents, and the daily routine involves more collaboration with colleagues in the area of educational activities. Their much greater involvement in extracurricular activities is an indication of wider educational objectives than the strictly academic ones. (Eighty-eight per cent of the English teachers were involved in at least one extracurricular activity, compared with only 31 per cent of French teachers.) The majority of English teachers performed considerably more than their basic teaching duties, while this was true of only a minority of the French teachers. It seems that the national context within which the educational system functions leads to a much wider conception of social role, either in the area of interaction (with colleagues and parents), or in the area of integration within wider socio-educational aims.

We also noted, as in the two previous chapters, that the location of the schools leads to interesting variations. For both cohorts, it is in the disadvantaged areas (inner-city zones) that contact with parents is the least frequent. However, this phenomenon is considerably more pronounced for the French cohort. In the same way, there is a greater lack of contact with social workers – quite a paradox in those areas where social problems represent by far the most disruptive factor affecting school progress.

To conclude, we present a brief 'identikit' profile which highlights some of the characteristics of a 'typical' French and a 'typical' English primary teacher.

A profile of Liz and Anne-Marie

Liz Grey is typical of the English primary teachers in our sample. She is in her mid- to late thirties, and has taught for 15 years, seven of them in her present school. She teaches a fourth-year junior class of 30 pupils in a school of 210 pupils.

If Liz is typical of the English primary teacher, Anne-Marie Dupont is typical of the French primary teachers in our sample. Although she is fairly close to Liz in terms of age and experience, in many ways the world in which Anne-Marie works is very different from the working conditions experienced by Liz. Anne-Marie is in her late thirties or early forties, works in a primary school in a suburb of Marseilles and has taught for over 20 years, about eight of them in her present school. At this point, however, the similarity ends. Anne-Marie teaches a class of only 22 pupils in a school of 170 pupils.

Like all French teachers, Anne-Marie has the status of a civil servant and, in exchange for security of employment, a pension and personal guarantees, is expected to accept, in theory at least, that the State is entitled to control, assess and sanction the manner in which the profession operates. Anne-Marie is not expected to perform such duties as registration or supervision of school meals, nor to stand in for absent colleagues.

The day-to-day life described by Liz and Anne-Marie reveals significant differences. Anne-Marie takes no part at all in extracurricular activities, and her colleagues who do run school clubs, workshops, choir, etc. are in the minority. She rarely works in close collaboration with her colleagues, but when she does, this mainly takes the form of an exchange of skills or groups of pupils.

In contrast, Liz expects to take part in organizing out-of-school activities and indeed sees it as an integral part of her work. She runs at least two school clubs each week. In her professional life she works frequently in close collaboration with colleagues, discussing work with them, and exchanging skills and groups. Anne-Marie has some difficulty in describing her 'teaching style'. It does not appear to be a concept with which she is familiar, but from an outsider's viewpoint it might be described as verging more towards the formal and traditional than that of her English colleagues.

There is a great divergence between the attitude of the French and English teachers towards the role of parents. Both Liz and Anne-Marie are in complete agreement that teachers as professionals are in a better position than parents to make decisions about curriculum and teaching methods. Both argue that teachers should not adapt their teaching (curriculum and methods) to meet parents' wishes, but that teachers do have a duty to explain the methods they use to parents. However, at this point they begin to diverge.

When it comes to her professional relationship with parents, Liz is much more likely than Anne-Marie to involve parents and to have parents actively participating in classroom activities. On the other hand, she sees parents less often to discuss a child's progress. She often takes parents' opinions into account when evaluating her work with pupils and sees this as an important way of assessing her teaching. In addition, she is very concerned with parents as an influence, although not *the* most important influence on her teaching practice, and she also has a strong feeling of responsibility in the sense of accountability towards parents.

Anne-Marie, on the other hand, rarely or never takes parents' opinions into account when evaluating her work with pupils and does not see this as an important way of assessing her work. For her, parents are not important as an influence on her teaching practice. She, too, feels a sense of responsibility and accountability towards parents, but less strongly than Liz; nor does she feel as convinced as Liz that teachers should be ready to listen to parents' opinions and be available to discuss personal matters with parents. She does, though, feel quite strongly that a child's progress in school is ultimately the responsibility of the teacher, whilst Liz disagrees with this, perhaps influenced by her consciousness of 'parent power'.

In the following chapter we fill out the details of this profile a little more by discussing the working environment of the teachers in the two countries and the way in which this relates to their classroom practice.

Chapter 6

Teachers' Working Environment and Classroom Practice

What are the characteristics of the schools in which the primary school teachers in France and England work? How similar are the buildings and their layout, and the individual classrooms? Does their use reflect similar working habits? Do teachers in each country work with similar class sizes and types of pupils? How do the teachers differ in their classroom practice, their organization and management? These are the questions with which this chapter attempts to deal on the basis both of the observations made during the authors' many classroom visits and of the quantitative information given by the teachers themselves.

THE SCHOOLS

The buildings

There are many similarities in the exterior of the school buildings visited in both countries. Both reflect a succession of new ideas in architecture from the turn of the century onwards, and it is noticeable that the differences between school buildings within one country are as great as the differences between the countries.

There are, however, clear differences in the internal organization of the buildings. In England, schools have more rooms allocated to uses other than standard classroom activities. All English schools have staffrooms and most have school halls which are used for assemblies and school gatherings as well as for physical education activities. In French schools there is at the most only one spare room, often small (described as multi-purpose), for all non-standard activities. These differences are an indicator of the much greater significance of collaboration and interchange of teachers and pupils in England as compared with France – a difference to which we shall return in subsequent chapters. Also, English classrooms and external areas such as corridors and entrance halls present a warmer, more friendly appearance because of the many decorations and exhibits of pupils' work. Schools in both countries have outdoor play areas, but in France a section of these, known as the *préau*, is often covered so that pupils can play games outside even in wet weather.

Table 6.1   *Number of pupils on roll*

Population	No. of pupils	No. of schools				
		Zone 1: rural	Zone 2: working-class	Zone 3: inner city	Zone 4: middle-class	Total
French	<25	11				11
	26–125	22	5	1	4	32
	126–200	7	7	9	8	31
	201–250		5	3	6	14
	251–300		2	2	2	6
	>300			1		
		40	19	16	20	94
English	<25	2				2
	26–125	21	1	6	3	31
	126–200	8	7	13	7	35
	201–250	2	6	2	5	15
	251–300		3	4	4	11
	>300			4	7	11
		33	17	29	26	105

School size

In both cohorts the number of pupils on the school roll varied considerably. At one extreme were schools with fewer than 25 pupils, and at other schools with more than 300. It will come as no great surprise that the small schools were in the majority of cases rural schools, which accounted for 77 per cent (France) and 70 per cent (England) of schools with fewer than 125 pupils; the large urban schools accounted for 100 per cent (France) and 95 per cent (England) of the schools involved in our study with more than 200 pupils.

Table 6.1, however, shows that very large schools were much more common in England than they were in France: in the county of Avon 11 schools out of the 105 studied had more than 300 pupils, whilst there was only one such school out of the 95 studied in the Académie d'Aix-Marseille. Conversely, very small schools (fewer than 25 pupils) were much more common in France than they were in England, accounting for 27.5 per cent of rural schools in France, but only 6 per cent of rural schools in England.

THE CLASSES

General overview

The classes involved in our study reflect exactly the general differences observed between the two countries and reported in Chapter 2. In the French classes that we visited, almost invariably the layout of the desks followed the classical pattern of the teacher's desk facing neat parallel rows of pupils' desks. We very rarely found the layout which is characteristic of the vast majority of English primary schools: desks or tables grouped together in a number of areas corresponding to different themes or activities, with the pupils sitting around the areas defined in this way, and the teacher

Table 6.2 *Class sizes*

Population	No. of pupils	Percentage of classes				
		Zone 1: rural	Zone 2: working-class	Zone 3: inner city	Zone 4: middle-class	Mean (%)
French	<15	15.8	4.8	6.1	1.0	6.9
	16–20	22.5	23.3	38.3	9.1	23.3
	21–25	41.5	46.7	42.4	52.5	45.8
	26–30	18.0	22.3	12.1	36.4	22.2
	>30	2.2	2.9	1.1	1.0	1.8
		100	100	100	100	100
English	<15	8.7	9.2	10.5	1.3	7.5
	16–20	10.0	2.6	10.5	–	5.8
	21–25	21.3	14.5	22.4	3.9	15.5
	26–30	37.5	35.5	35.5	34.3	35.7
	>30	22.5	38.2	21.1	60.5	35.5
		100	100	100	100	100

often moving between the groups. In the French cohort, the very few classes which had that layout were most often classes run by a teacher who had adopted a different pedagogical philosophy (Freinet's, for instance), or classes with a special purpose (remedial classes for pupils from underprivileged areas in a 'ZEP' – *zone d'éducation prioritaire* – for instance). The choice of different working methods, which affects both the objectives and the running of the class, here leads the teacher to adopt a layout that is different from the standard one.

Class size

General remarks

A comparison between French and English classes reveals so many important differences that it hardly needs a commentary. A quick glance at Table 6.2 will reveal that, whatever the geographic zone, the numbers of pupils per class were much higher in English schools than in French schools. The average for both of our cohorts was 22.3 pupils per class in France and 27.5 in England, which means, on average, 4.2 more pupils in English classrooms.

The difference is even more striking if we consider the spread of classes according to their size. Whatever the zone considered, there were many more small classes, and fewer large classes, in the French cohort. Thirty per cent of French classes had a maximum of 20 pupils, as opposed to only 13 per cent in the English cohort. Also, only 24 per cent of French classes (as opposed to 71 per cent of the English classes in our study) had more than 25 pupils. If we consider only the very large classes, the difference was even more striking: there were more than 30 pupils in at least one in three English classes (36 per cent), whilst in France this was exceptional (fewer than 2 per cent of classes). It is ironic that, in England, teachers are attempting to practise an individualized pedagogy with class sizes far larger than those with which the French teacher works in a formal, didactic way. Clearly, the situation is likely to be easier for the teacher in France, where since 1975 a number of governmental measures have led to a decrease in class size.

The role played by the location of the schools

In both countries, it was in the affluent middle-class zones (Zone 4) where the largest classes were to be found. In Aix-Marseille 37 per cent of classes in the middle-class areas had more than 25 pupils, whilst only one in ten (10 per cent) had 20 or less. The very same phenomenon can be observed in the English cohort. In the county of Avon it was also in the affluent middle-class areas that the classes were the largest, to such an extent that 95 per cent of classes had more than 25 pupils, and 60 per cent more than 30. And in those areas only one class in 100 (1 per cent) had 20 pupils or less.

In both countries, it is in the inner city that there are proportionately more moderately sized classes and fewer large classes. In both countries too the greatest contrast is between the affluent middle-class areas and the inner city, while the greatest similarity is between rural areas (Zone 1) and inner-city areas (Zone 3).

The contrast between the affluent middle-class areas and the inner-city areas in both countries may be explained in similar ways. The attractive nature of schools in affluent middle-class areas leads a certain number of parents living on the periphery of those areas to try to get their children into those schools. Their success in this depends on whether the regulations (official or not) relating to the location of the residence carry much weight or are respected to the letter. In the county of Avon, where there were few geographical restrictions regarding the choice of school at the time of the study, this phenomenon reached maximum proportions. And it is still very much apparent in the region around Marseilles, despite a fairly strict allocation of school places according to residence. Parental pressure leads to exceptions being made.

The relatively small size of classes in the less well-off inner-city areas (Zone 3) can also be explained by the educational policies in both countries. An undeniable effort has been made during the past two decades to improve teaching conditions in this respect. In England there has been a particularly marked policy of allocating a more favourable teacher–pupil ratio to such schools.

The scholastic progress of the pupils

The progress of the pupils

Table 6.3 gives very general information on the way in which the schoolchildren from both our cohorts progress through school. The differences emphasize the extent to which educational policies differ in the two countries. In France, at the time of the study, the policy of *redoublement* (repeating the year) was still being implemented for pupils judged not to have reached the required level. This was despite often voiced reservations and criticisms, both in educational and in psychological circles (see, for instance, Gilly, 1967), and the wishes of the educational authorities since the Haby reform in 1975. Twenty-nine per cent of all primary school pupils in our study had repeated at least a year. Nineteen per cent had repeated one year (thus being 1 year behind their age mates) and 10 per cent had repeated two years (being therefore 2 years behind). For a French pupil, progress in school is rather like running an obstacle

Table 6.3 *Percentage of pupils in advance, at the legal age, and behind by one or two years*

Population	Relative progress	Percentage of pupils				
		Zone 1: rural	Zone 2: working-class	Zone 3: inner city	Zone 4: middle-class	Mean (%)
French	In advance	2.1	1.8	1.9	4.4	2.6
	Legal age	75.6	66.7	47.8	80.9	68.0
	1 yr behind	15.6	21.2	28.7	11.1	19.1
	2 yrs behind	6.7	10.3	21.6	3.6	10.3
		100	100	100	100	100
English	In advance	5.3	3.5	3.7	4.1	3.9
	Legal age	87.6	92.9	92.6	93.0	91.5
	1 yr behind	4.5	3.1	2.7	2.4	3.1
	2 yrs behind	2.4	1.0	1.0	1.0	1.3
		100	100	100	100	100

course: the first obstacle has to be tackled successfully before the pupil is allowed to tackle the next one. Being allowed into the next higher class is usually possible only if the pupil has reached the level corresponding to the norm-referenced objectives for the class in which he has just spent a year.

In England, the situation is quite different in that pupils never repeat a year. They all move on to secondary school at age 11, whilst in France the *redoublement* system means that it is possible for pupils to be entering secondary school at 12, 13 or, exceptionally, 14 years old.

Where our data indicate a small proportion (4.4 per cent) of English pupils who were 'behind' by a year, this is very often because they were in small rural schools where mixed age groups of pupils were kept together in one class owing to the small numbers of pupils in each age group. Sometimes with such mixed-age groupings 'vertical age groupings' are also set up for pedagogical reasons.

If the difference between French and English schools is so dramatic, it is quite simply because the underlying pedagogical principles are very different. In England, at the time of our study, progress at school was not dependent, at every stage, on norm-referenced criteria relating to knowledge, and defined by an official national curriculum imposed by an outside body. Every year each school established and adjusted, on its own initiative, its own curriculum and progression. It follows that the objectives defined were established much more on the basis of the true level of the pupils than on the basis of theoretical levels which are assumed to be typical of average pupils for the different ages, as is the case in France. It seems therefore reasonable to assume that there was less discrepancy in England between the objectives proposed and the average abilities of the pupils than is the case in France, where a considerable body of research has over a period of years stressed the unreasonable nature of the expected learning objectives (see, for instance, Gilly, 1967). Will this still be the case in the years to come? Will there still be no repeating of years in English primary schools? The question arises because the introduction of the National Curriculum, as a result of the 1988 Education Reform Act, may eventually lead to such a measure being necessary for those pupils who fail to reach the nationally imposed objectives.

Table 6.4 *Teachers' assessment of pupils' academic level*

Population	Academic level	Percentage of teachers				
		Zone 1: rural	Zone 2: working-class	Zone 3: inner city	Zone 4: middle-class	Mean (%)
French	Above average	16.5	16.9	7.8	24.9	16.8
	Average	61.5	58.1	48.2	58.8	56.8
	Below average	22.0	25.0	44.0	16.3	26.4
		100	100	100	100	100
English	Above average	24.8	17.9	10.3	35.7	22.3
	Average	53.9	46.5	37.3	45.1	45.7
	Below average	21.5	35.6	52.4	19.2	31.9
		100	100	100	100	100

Estimated level of the pupils

The consequences for pupils' progress of the different educational policies practised in the two countries naturally go hand in hand with differences in the working conditions of the teachers, and the way in which they manage their classes. We saw (Table 6.2) that the teacher in England normally has much larger classes than her French counterpart. In the absence of a policy of systematic elimination of the weaker pupils at the end of the school year, classes in England are certainly much more heterogeneous regarding level. At least, this seems to be the conclusion that should be drawn from Table 6.4, which presents a subjective evaluation by the teachers of the levels attained by their pupils in relation to the teachers' assessment of the general 'average' level of pupils for that particular year.

First of all, it is clear from the last column of Table 6.4 that, on the whole, both English and French teachers were pleased with the level of their pupils. When they gave an opinion on the average level of their class, the English teachers were even slightly more satisfied than the French teachers, but the difference was so small to be negligible. However, if the difference is negligible when talking of averages, this was definitely not the case when considering the spread of the assessments. Whatever the zone considered, this spread was much bigger for the English cohort than it was for the French cohort. If the assessments made are a true reflection of the real level of the pupils, then the heterogeneity of English classes is considerably greater. This has clear implications for the management of the classes. It would be far less easy for the English teacher to treat the class as a homogeneous group for all teaching purposes. Certainly the format of the formal presentation by the teacher followed by practical exercises is not a commonly used practice in English schools as it is in French schools. English teachers are much more likely to practise small-group teaching than their French counterparts, as we shall see later on in this chapter.

Not surprisingly, in both countries it is in the affluent middle-class areas where teachers feel most satisfied with the level attained by their pupils, and in the inner city where the estimated level is lowest. This is despite the existence of larger class sizes, particularly in English middle-class areas.

CLASSROOM PRACTICE

The different institutional characteristics reported in the preceding sections are closely related to the striking differences in classroom organization and management which we report here. The observations which follow are based upon the shadowing of 16 teachers in each country for up to a week at a time, using field notes and a systematic observation schedule.

This investigation revealed striking differences in pedagogy, in classroom organization and in teacher–pupil relations, which were far greater between the two countries than any of the differences observed *within* one country (for example in schools located in different socio-economic catchment areas).

Pedagogy

Particularly evident were different practices of differentiation and grouping, a differing emphasis in the two countries on the acquisition of principles and concepts compared with an emphasis on knowledge acquired through rote learning, and a different value placed on the product of learning as opposed to the process.

In most English classrooms there were typically three or four different activities going on at the same time; in France this was very rarely seen, much of the teaching being didactic and centred on one activity for the whole class. English teachers were also more likely to divide the class into groups and to use attainment level as a basis for this division and for differentiated approaches in their teaching. A much greater tendency to relate teaching to perceived pupil and group need was apparent in English classrooms than in French ones because, for the most part, French pupils were typically engaged in the same task for most of the time. Nevertheless, even in England teachers often maintained a high degree of control over the pacing of children's tasks.

Teachers in England, because of their greater need to maintain individual contact and to supervise groups, were much more likely to move around the class looking at children's work, helping and giving instruction and direction, whereas French teachers were typically on the platform or on a stool at the front of the class, as might be expected for a more 'whole-class' pedagogy. Reading provides another example of these differences. Whilst English teachers, typically, heard children read individually, French teachers commonly had children read around the class. In England the whole approach was typically found to be much more active and emphasized discovery-based learning. The teacher often appeared to be encouraging creative thinking, whereas in France the effort was more likely to be directed towards leading children to the correct answer.

Thus teachers in England were more likely to use questions in a way that built upon children's responses until the desired result was achieved, whilst French teachers would typically reject a child's response if it was not exactly what they wanted.

For example, one teacher in England, doing language work with a small group, asked 'What are sentences?' The children made various attempts at an answer, including 'bits of writing' and 'writing put together'.

> *Teacher*: 'So it's a piece of writing, isn't it? Strings of what?'
> *Children*: 'Words.'
> *Teacher*: 'A string of words that makes sense. If I said to you "In the sky", is that a sentence?'
> *Children*: 'No.'

Teacher: '"There's a bird in the sky" is a sentence, isn't it? What does it end with?'
Children: 'A full stop.'

In one school in France, the teacher took in children's books where the children had been asked to write a complete sentence.

Teacher (looking through books): 'This is not a sentence, this is not a sentence either, neither is this. This looks, smells and tastes like a sentence, but it is not one. It's wrong. A sentence has to use existing words and in the right order. Marc, read us your sentence using "champignons".'
Marc: 'J'ai mangé des champignons.'
Teacher: 'It's not wrong, in fact it's correct, but it's boring.'

The teacher then gave more examples of sentences, and went on to analyse the objects of each sentence.

On balance, English teachers appeared to be concerned to encourage creativity and inventiveness, giving clear priority to the understanding of principles and concepts. French teachers in contrast placed a strong emphasis on acquiring knowledge through rote learning and were more concerned to achieve pupils' conformity to a common goal. Suggestions from pupils in some cases were not often welcomed or used, and typically much less sought after than in England. Creative writing was consequently an important feature in English school, whilst in French schools there was more emphasis on grammar and analysis of sentence structure as well as on poetry recitation skills. Children often worked extensively with dictionaries, concentrating on definitions of words. However, evidence of genuine open-ended discussion was rare in both countries.

In summary, the pedagogy of many primary classrooms in France seemed to be characterized by an emphasis on the product rather than the process of learning. There was a strong emphasis on reaching the correct answer as quickly as possible, and neatness and attractive, well-set-out exercise books and impressive pieces of finished work were highly valued. In England generally, more stress was laid on the learning process and less on the finished product, with teachers differentiating work according to level and breadth to meet pupils' perceived capabilities.

By contrast, the main aim of virtually all the French teachers observed was for all pupils to achieve the same basic standard in order to meet the objectives set by the end of the year. Work was paced to conform to the level of the middle group. Those who could proceed faster were unlikely to be permitted to undertake work at a higher level.

Classroom organization and teacher–pupil relations

Because of the variety of activities and the individualized pedagogy, queuing at the teacher's desk was a constant feature of many English classroom, whilst it occurred rarely, if at all, in France. Consequently there was more apparent time-wasting of children in England and less apparent application to work. Although some teachers in England showed great awareness of queuing as a problem and used strategies to cut it down, there were obvious limitations to such possibilities. Thus whilst English pupils experienced considerably more feedback of a concurrent kind than their French counterparts, the corollary of this was frequently delay and some pupils getting more help than others.

In France the level of participation of pupils was generally very high, and here too we observed more constant pressure on the part of teachers to secure pupils' work and effort, whilst there were far more instances in England of lapses of concentration and lack of pupil effort being unchallenged by the teacher.

The typical approach in French classrooms was to encourage pupils to work on their own without helping each other. Sometimes children were told to work with satchels on the desk between them to hide their work from other children. Occasionally slates were used so that children could write the correct answer on them and then hold them up to show the teacher. In one classroom, a boy was called to the front of the class to recite his five times table all the way through. The teacher insisted that he do this alone without help from other children, and when he got stuck the teacher became angry at the number of children calling out answers, saying that the first who spoke would be punished. The boy was sent back to his place and told that he would have to repeat the task the next day.

In contrast, most English teachers encouraged children to work co-operatively for much of the time. This meant that children were likely to be free to move around the room, and to seek other pupils and resources, even outside the classroom, whilst in France pupils were often rooted to their desks. Consequently the English classrooms were often characterized by children talking much of the time while French classrooms were likely to be relatively quiet and undisturbed.

Both groups of teachers showed considerable pleasure in the act of teaching with many in both countries showing sympathetic interest in pupils and enthusiasm in their teaching. However, teachers in England had to work much harder at maintaining discipline, whilst in France, where teacher–pupil relations were more formal and the level of control generally stricter, teachers appeared to need to exercise that control far less frequently. Often a mere glance was enough to quell deviant behaviour.

In English classrooms relations between teacher and pupil were warmer and more informal, there was also considerable evidence of teachers striving to protect and encourage pupils' self-esteem by using praise both of pupils and their work. Criticism of children's work and even calling them names was very noticeable in France, with most positive reinforcement being used in the inner-city areas. It was also common in England for children to be discouraged from commenting on each other's mistakes, while in France this sometimes appeared to be encouraged implicitly by teachers. In one class we observed the teacher went from desk to desk commenting to the whole class, 'C'est bon', 'C'est mauvais' about children's work, with accompanying gasps from the rest of the class. One boy was told in front of others that he had made serious mistakes and that he would probably have to *redouble* (repeat the year).

In practice, teachers in France appeared to take one of two roles, either that of parent or that of dictator. In England there was typically a third dimension: teacher as colleague or facilitator, allowing children to make their own decisions and supporting their learning.

Summary of classroom practice

Thus in summary it may be said that a number of the factors which research suggests to be positive features in teaching, such as teacher warmth, sensitivity to pupils, an emphasis on pupils' positive achievements, working towards pupils' achievement of self-control and autonomy, were all more often observed in England than in France. In England also there were a greater variety of activities going on in the classroom, more variation of treatment according to pupil needs, more emphasis on teaching for understanding and more concurrent feedback to pupils.

However, these features, which would appear to most English teachers as desirable, seemed sometimes to be achieved at the expense of an orderly, calm classroom and perhaps of a good working environment. We have reported more evidence in England of pupils avoiding work and of teachers being unaware of what was going on in the class as a whole. There was also more evidence of teacher anxiety and tension. Whereas in France most of the teachers observed controlled the class easily and effectively, this was less true in England, although, as noted above, these observations need to be seen in the context of an average class size in the English classrooms of 30 and in France of 22. Thus, ironically, English teachers are typically working with an ideology of child-centredness and attention to the individual in the context of a class size much larger than that of the French teacher, who is aiming at whole-class teaching and an undifferentiated pedagogy in which the size of the class is much less significant.

It is important to emphasize that French teachers believe strongly in the need for a national curriculum as the basis for equality and unity in their society. More immediately, however, they feel an overwhelming pressure to meet the attainment targets laid down for children by the end of the year. That strong sense of obligation to equip children with the skills and knowledge expected from a particular year grade so that they will not be forced to *redouble* is the source of much of the conformity, the emphasis on rote learning, the didactic teaching methods and the lack of response to perceived variations in pupil needs indentified in our observations.

OVERVIEW AND SUMMARY

The data analysed in this chapter showed that there are clear differences in the way school buildings and classrooms are organized in France and England. The English schools we studied have more rooms reserved for special purposes such as staffrooms and assembly halls, and the layout of their classrooms favours group work around specific themes. This merely reflects the general differences mentioned in Chapter 2.

The quantitative data analysed also revealed important differences. In England, large schools are more numerous, and the average class size is much bigger. Finally, whilst in England entry into the next higher class at the beginning of a new school year is automatic, regardless of the location of the school, the progress of French schoolchildren is often (for almost 30 per cent of the cohort) halted by the repeating of at least one year, this being the case particularly for children from disadvantaged areas. The lack of elimination in English schools of the 'less able' children from one school year to the next leads to a greater spread of levels (as judged by the teachers). However, this greater spread does not mean that the English teachers are less satisfied with the average level of their pupils than their French counterparts.

It would certainly seem to the outside observer looking afresh at both systems that working conditions in English schools are rather less good than they are in French schools: larger schools, larger classes and a greater spread of levels. At the same time, English teachers are attempting to deliver an individualized and child-centred pedagogy.

However, it is important to bear in mind that at the time of the study, the English primary school teachers did not share with their French counterparts a fear of pupils' not reaching the prescribed objectives, and of being held responsible for the failure of those pupils. This fundamental difference between the two systems, which resides in the freedom of the teacher to determine the nature of the objectives to be reached, is essential to an understanding of teachers' responses. It is clear that reasons of economy rather than educational policy are the determining factors in the size of the classes, but it is hard to see how the English teacher could handle satisfactorily the numbers and the varied levels of her pupils if she did not have a certain degree of freedom in the exact details of the curriculum to be followed. A system which on the whole does not have official norm-referenced stages allows for a better handling of individual differences, and quite naturally leads to a pupil-targeted approach on the part of the teachers. On the other hand, the focusing on norm-referenced objectives chosen by an outside body leads to set teaching methods, based on the formal lesson directed at the whole class. This is what happens in France, despite real efforts to get the teachers to take into account individual pupils instead of treating their class as a monolithic entity. There is in fact an incompatibility between norm-referenced objectives imposed by an outside body, and the possibility of adopting truly pupil-oriented teaching methods. This latter type of approach is possible within a class only if the principle of different levels for different pupils at the end of the school year is accepted. However, such a principle is fundamentally in disagreement with the norm-referenced objectives prescribed by the official programmes. There would seem to be a strong argument for taking into account the differences between individual pupils from the outset, rather than becoming obsessed by the awesome task of having to get all the pupils to learn the same thing. With such a system, it ought to be possible to organize the class in such a way that each pupil can learn at his own speed, and make the most of the objectives proposed; as a consequence, the pupils' new knowledge will be acquired on a more solid basis than if the same speed of acquisition, and the same testing requirements, had been imposed on all pupils.

One of the problems associated with the introduction of the National Curriculum in England without an accompanying reduction in class size is clear. How will teachers be able to carry on with such varied attainment levels in their class unless, eventually, a system of repeating the year is introduced?

An analysis of the teachers' assessment of the level of their pupils shows that both French and English teachers make a close link between social class and scholastic achievement. Moreover, our data confirm that in both countries the educational authorities aim for smaller classes in disadvantaged areas. It would be interesting to carry the comparison further. How do schools tackle inequalities caused by social class in a system where repeating a year is standard practice and in a system where it isn't, and what are the comparative consequences of the measures taken to that effect? If more information were available than is the case with the present study, this would make a most interesting topic for further research. We shall, however, see that some of the information reported in Chapter 7 reveals the existence of a number of further differences in how teachers perceive their practice, which cannot be explained without reference to the fundamental differences in educational policy which we have been discussing.

Part III

How Teachers See Their Work

Part III of the book is based on an analysis of those parts of the questionnaire which asked the teachers to express opinions. The data collected concern the teachers' perception of their work, with an emphasis, as mentioned already, on their conception of the primary school teacher's role and of their professional responsibilities.

We start by examining the teachers' professional perspectives which emerged from two general questions on teachers' work and professional responsibility. In subsequent chapters the differences which are revealed between the two countries are analysed further, around the three themes: for which particular educational objectives do the teachers feel most responsible? What are the influences and constraints on their practice, and what degree of freedom do they perceive themselves as having when they exercise their responsibilities? Finally, to whom do they feel they are accountable?

Following the pattern used in Part II, the focus for Part III will be the comparison between the two countries. If there appear to be differences linked to the location of the schools, we shall always attempt to find out whether this difference is identical for both groups.

Chapter 7

The Meaning of 'Professionalism'

In this and the following three chapters we approach the heart of the study – what professional responsibility means to teachers – by examining how teachers themselves talk spontaneously about their work when their responses are not pre-structured in any way by the research design. Since the discussion here is based on responses to an open-ended question asking teachers 'What does professional responsibility mean to you?' (question 18), it is appropriate to allow the quotations from teachers to speak for themselves as far as possible within a framework of analysis which attempts to make sense both of the considerable differences between teachers in the two countries *and* between different teachers within each country. We go on to analyse complementary data in which teachers were asked to agree or disagree with a number of statements about the nature of teaching as work.

BEING PROFESSIONALLY RESPONSIBLE

When asked to describe what professional responsibility meant to them, many of the teachers wrote lengthy replies averaging half a page, which posed a considerable challenge in categorizing and interpreting the data. No pre-determined analytic framework was imposed on the responses. The lack of a concept of accountability in France and of any policy debate on the subject meant that it was difficult to establish analytic categories relevant to the two sets of responses. Consequently the French and English researchers had to work closely together at every stage of data analysis, as described in Chapter 4. Our purpose in this chapter will be merely to discuss general features, with a view to presenting a more in-depth study of selected aspects of the replies in the following chapters.

Four dimensions of responsibility

For both French and English teachers, four main dimensions of responsibility emerge (Table 7.1). The teachers talked of accountability to others, objectives to be reached in their teaching and ways of teaching, but they also mentioned areas which go beyond

Table 7.1   *The meaning of professional responsibility: percentage of teachers mentioning each of the four dimensions*

Dimension	Teachers	
	French	English
Accountability to whom?	88.4%	92.3%
Responsibility for attaining objectives in relation to pupils	72.3%	82.7%
Responsibility for areas of teaching	45.6%	76.5%
Meta-professional considerations	58.5%	67.5%

purely academic responsibilities (these might be called meta-professional responsibilities); that is, the need to reflect upon the role of the teacher within society. The difference between the two cohorts is striking. On the whole, the English teachers provided far more detailed replies. More of the teachers from the English cohort mentioned one of the four categories above, and also all of those categories. The notion of professional responsibility appeared to be far more complex for the English teachers than for the French, and they were particularly concerned with the need to reflect upon the nature of their role and how to carry it out.

Nevertheless, for both cohorts the dimension of 'accountability to other' is the most common: for approximately 90 per cent of the teachers, professional responsibility meant being responsible or answerable to someone (oneself and/or others) or to various bodies. The notion of professional responsibility therefore implied in the majority of cases the notion of accountability. It also implied in many cases objectives to be reached, although this came in second place only, and varied in importance according to the country, since this was mentioned in 83 per cent of the replies for the English cohort, as opposed to 72 per cent for the French cohort. This variation was even more marked for the third category: for more than three English teachers in every four (77 per cent) professional responsibility also implied ways of teaching, whilst this was the case for not quite one French teacher in every two (46 per cent).

Finally, after this brief overview, let us explain what we mean by meta-professional responsibilities, which were mentioned far more often by the English cohort (68 per cent) than by the French cohort (59 per cent). Equal numbers of teachers in the two cohorts (approximately one-third) mentioned aspects of 'being a professional' (doing one's job properly, meeting one's contractual responsibility, acting in a professional manner, doing one's job to the best of one's abilities). Many teachers, although not quite as many as above (roughly one in ten), said that they must act as a model for the pupils. Still fewer teachers (roughly one in 20) said that they must be able to look at their own performance as teachers in a critical or reflective fashion.

French teachers, on the whole, appeared to be more certain about the exact nature of the teacher's responsibilities, and had a much more precise idea of what their duties were than the English teachers. Whilst the French cohort had a tendency to see the teacher's job more in personal terms, the English teachers tended to see professional responsibility as an involvement of the whole person, a 'commitment of self' (Nias, 1989). More English teachers had a broad conception of the nature of their job in terms of relationships with others (both colleagues and other partners in the education process) (18 per cent compared with 4 per cent). They were more likely to talk of their duty to support and speak in defence of the profession within society (11 per cent compared with 3 per cent in France), and finally more of them felt that professional responsibility implies a duty to try constantly to keep abreast of current developments and practices, and to improve their expertise (15 per cent compared with 7 per cent).

The underlying conceptions

Two very different conceptions of the nature of teaching emerge from these responses. At one extreme is a broad conception, which involves the sharing of responsibilities and an outlook on the outside world which puts more emphasis on the teaching process than on results, and carries a fair amount of uncertainty. The other extreme is a narrow conception, which implies that teachers feel personally responsible and have little interest in the outside world, and puts more emphasis on the concrete results of teaching than on the learning processes. This involves relatively little uncertainty. There are many different positions between these two extremes, and the difference between the two countries is not totally clear-cut. It is evident, however, that most English teachers hold a conception of teaching which corresponds to the broader or extended notion of responsibility, whilst most of the French teachers hold a conception which corresponds with the narrower or 'restricted' notion of responsibility (Hoyle, 1980).

In the narrow conception of the teacher's job, which is rather more typical of the French cohort, teaching practices are based mostly on personal involvement and individual experience, and are focused on the classroom. The replies emphasize the essentially classroom-centred role of the teacher, and her responsibility for attaining school results and achieving objectives. It is a conception which revolves around the teacher, and carries strong moral connotations, although at the same time it is very dependent on external norms for the definition of the objectives to be reached. For instance, a French teacher says, 'to me, being professionally responsible means doing one's job to the best of one's ability given the official curriculum, and attempting to follow this curriculum as closely as possible. Being responsible means rejecting carelessness.' Other replies are even more succinct, like those of three French teachers for whom being professionally responsible means 'doing the required job to the best of one's ability', or 'doing one's job, not being absent, following the official curriculum', or again 'following the official curriculum, that is putting the defined objectives into practice in my class'.

Within the broad conception, which is rather more typical of the English teachers, professional responsibility is not restricted to reaching strictly academic objectives. It includes objectives other than school results, and often refers to extracurricular activities. The notion of responsibility towards parents, the local community and colleagues is rather more important than the notion of responsibility towards oneself and the hierarchy. For instance, an English teacher writes, 'I'm responsible to each child in my class, that he/she develops intellectually, socially and emotionally during the time in my class. Also I'm responsible to the children's parents that they are informed of the problems and needs of their child, and have some say in how their child is treated in my class.' The conception already discussed of the teacher's job being a lonely one is replaced by a conception which is based on dialogue and collaboration with colleagues. For instance, an English teacher who talks of professional responsibility says: 'In my work I must work closely with others to help the mental, physical, creative and moral development of the children in my care. These people will be most importantly parents followed by other teachers, social workers, psychologists, etc.' Another English teacher says, 'being professionally responsible means working with my colleagues to achieve our goals for the children . . . consultation with head and senior staff. Making myself available for consultation with parents whenever I/they feel it necessary.' And a third teacher says, 'to be caring for both teaching and non-teaching staff and to give support when and where needed. To be a good PR man – to be approachable by parents. To enjoy and care for my children in school.'

The wide objectives which are characteristic of the broad (or extended) conception of the teacher's role go hand in hand with the feeling of belonging to an educational community which has an important role to play, with its own share of the responsibility, and to which one is accountable. This conception also frequently implies a striving to improve one's teaching practice by seeking help from external sources such as reading, in-service courses, etc., as opposed to the narrow (or restricted) conception which sees possible improvements as being the result of personal experience. For instance, an English teacher says:

> professional responsibility means instructing the children, making sure of their well-being at school, being involved in everything that concerns the children by taking part in the upkeep and development of the school together with the local community, and by improving my professional expertise; creating a cooperative environment where each child can develop and become a responsible adult.

Another English teacher says:

> I must always be aware of new techniques by going on courses, reading educational publications, etc. I try to bring these to the attention of my colleagues by discussion and, once again, example. . . . I need to feel satisfied with my teaching – and to do this I have to put into my work a lot of thought, planning, etc. I thoroughly enjoy the interaction with other teachers I meet on courses – I find the necessary 'drug' to bring enthusiasm and enjoyment into my teaching.

The conscientiousness, the commitment, even the enthusiasm manifest in the above replies are also present in the narrow, more restricted conception of the teacher's role, although there is no sign of the concern for broader educational aims. For one French teacher, being professionally responsible means

> to make sure that my pupils acquire the knowledge and skills necessary for the passage into the next class up. To avoid error in the evaluation of my pupils. To remain as far as possible attentive to their needs and expectations whilst at the same time remaining objective and unassuming in my role as teacher.

For another French teacher it means, 'to evaluate my work conscientiously, and to be responsible for the quality of my teaching'. For a third French teacher it means 'to work as carefully and conscientiously as possible, but also enthusiastically, to encourage the learning of the children who are entrusted to us for six hours of the day'. The emphasis placed on commitment and conscientiousness even leads one French teacher to go as far as saying:

> teaching is probably one of the professions which carries the most responsibility; each teacher is responsible for the destiny of all, not merely from the point of view of academic results, but also from the point of view of the individual's intellectual, moral and social development.

The commitment combined with the narrowness of the conception often leads to a kind of exacerbation of a sense of personal responsibility whenever there is a failure. If the teacher feels personally responsible, she cannot but find herself at fault:

> being responsible means being responsible towards oneself, never blaming the pupils, society, the curriculum, exclusively for any failure, but being able to question one's teaching practices .

> (a French teacher)

a failure can always be put down to the teacher despite any extenuating circumstances; even if a child is unable to read because of previous bad teaching, or because of the family situation, I feel that I have failed if I have been unable to teach that child something, both on the professional and the personal level.

(another French teacher)

The broad outlook, on the other hand, together with the collaboration that it entails, often leads to a lessening of the feeling of personal responsibility. The teacher is no longer solely responsible for any failure; she feels that the responsibility is shared with several members of a team.

There is no doubt that these differences, summed up by the notion of an 'extended' conception of responsibility in England and a 'restricted' conception in France, reflect in great measure the differences in the two educational systems. The French system, with its high degree of centralization, the defining of specific educational objectives for each school year by a national body, and the consequent practice of making children repeat a year when they do not reach the expected standard (see Chapter 5), leads the teacher to focus on strictly academic objectives, and to emphasize the personal nature of her responsibility in the contract which binds her to the hierarchical body controlling the profession. This is achieved at the expense of a close relationship with local partners (colleagues and parents), and of a sharing of responsibilities. But at the same time the highly standardized institutional constraints (concerning the objectives to be reached and the amount of control exercised) which apply to the teacher and also to all members of the profession bring a degree of structure and security. The feeling of belonging to a group, which is clearly defined through the rules that specify its function and the way it works, can therefore explain to an extent why French teachers more often demonstrate more certainty as to the precise nature of their role. The search for a precise conception of the teacher's role is all the more necessary since, although they belong to a well-structured group, teachers feel isolated regarding their professional responsibility.

Conversely, the highly decentralized English system (at the time of the study), with schools mainly financed and controlled by local authorities, and characterized by a great degree of freedom in defining the curriculum, led the teachers to work together with other colleagues, and to be more open to the local community (parents and colleagues particularly), hence the broad outlook that is manifest in the conception of the teacher's role and responsibilities. It is not surprising that such an extended conception, implying as it does a degree of freedom and a sharing of responsibilities, should lead to a certain amount of uncertainty. This is because it is difficult, when deprived of the security afforded by official programmes and instructions, to be absolutely sure about the objectives to be chosen, and the best way to reach them. As one English teacher put it:

A teacher can feel responsible to so many people, or groups of people, that s/he may well end up feeling responsible to no one, or differently to different people in turn, and very often it is the kids one is teaching that come out the worst.

Another inner-city English teacher talked of 'the triangle of tensions at times invigorating and at other times almost overpowering' that the primary teacher experiences in feeling sometimes conflicting responsibilities to so many different groups of people. However, although there is a bigger element of doubt in the extended conception, this element may be easier to cope with, since it applies to all teachers, and since any teacher can therefore find support from colleagues whenever there are uncertainties.

There is no doubt that the differences in the length and type of training received by teachers in the two countries (see Chapter 5) also contribute to the formation of these 'restricted' and 'extended' conceptions of teachers' work. However, the organization of teacher education is in itself a product of the fundamentally different pedagogical models which underlie the two educational systems.

BEING A TEACHER

In the second part of this chapter we move on to consider teachers' responses when asked to agree or disagree with a series of statements about the nature of teaching (question 27). The teachers were presented with the following descriptions of teaching, derived partly from statements made by teachers themselves in both countries, and partly from previous research: 'For me, teaching 1. is a vocation; 2. is a means of earning a living like any other; 3. is collaboration in a creative endeavour with my colleagues; 4. is the daily pleasure of contact with children; 5. is a way of giving meaning to my life; 6. is a very hard job; 7. is a daily challenge; 8. is to do a job which is little valued by society; 9. gives me the chance of interesting social relationships; 10. means being isolated in my work.'

Whilst this question was clearly not intended to evoke the wealth of data which resulted from the previous open-ended question, it has the advantage of allowing for a more precise quantitative analysis. The results of this analysis confirm, on the one hand, the differences noted between the two countries and, on the other, point to a number of differences linked to the location of the schools, at least for the French cohort.

General overview

Figure 7.1 gives an overview, ignoring socio-economic zone differences, of the proportion of English and French teachers who agreed (completely and to some extent) with the various statements. The statements are listed in decreasing order of agreement so far as the French teachers are concerned.

If we consider initially only the more general trends, without taking into account the possible differences linked to the location of the schools, it is clear that there is some similarity in the ranking of the statements according to the degree of agreement expressed for both cohorts (0.75 Spearman's rho). For both cohorts, statements 6 and 4 were among the three statements with which teachers were most commonly in agreement: over 90 per cent of all the teachers felt that 'teaching is a very hard job', and that on the other hand it is also 'the daily pleasure of contact with children'. Most of the teachers of both cohorts also agreed, although to a lesser extent, that teaching is 'a daily challenge', and that this job, which is 'little valued by society', is 'a vocation'. On the other hand, both cohorts were least likely to agree with the statement that 'teaching is a means of earning a living like any other', 'teaching gives me the chance of interesting social relationships', and 'teaching means being isolated in my work'.

However, this similarity between the two cohorts is only relative, and must not be allowed to hide the existence of important differences, both in the proportion of agreement for each statement and in the ranking of these statements. In fact the English

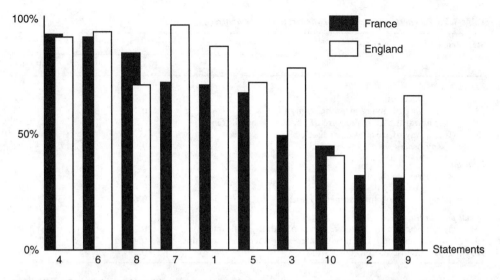

Figure 7.1 Perceptions of teaching: percentage of teachers in agreement with each of the following statements: 4, Teaching is the pleasure of daily contact with children; 6, Teaching is a very hard job; 8, Teaching is a job little valued by society; 7, Teaching is a daily challenge; 1, Teaching is a vocation; 5, Teaching is a way of giving meaning to my life; 3, Teaching is collaboration with my colleagues; 10, Teaching means being isolated in my work; 2, Teaching is a means of earning a living like any other; 9, Teaching gives the chance of interesting social relationships

teachers emphasized more frequently the fact that teaching is a hard job. Ninety-seven per cent as opposed to 72 per cent said that it is 'a daily challenge', and also felt that it is a vocation (89 per cent compared with 77 per cent). As for the French teachers, there was a larger proportion (86 per cent compared with 71 per cent) who felt that it is 'a job which is little valued by society'. On the other hand, considerably fewer of the French teachers felt that teaching is 'a means of earning a living like any other' (33 per cent compared with 58 per cent), that it is 'collaboration in a creative endeavour with my colleagues' (49 per cent compared with 79 per cent), or that it 'gives me the chance of interesting social relationships' (32 per cent compared with 68 per cent).

To summarize, within the very general common context of a job which is felt to be difficult, and which demands a vocation, the English teacher's conception is characterized by the perceived need for permanent reflection and striving (daily challenge), and for a collaborative effort to find solutions to the problems. Also these teachers feel less distant, less cut off from the real world, since more of them feel that teaching is a means of earning a living like any other, and that it gives them interesting social relationships. Again, these replies are more characteristic of a more open conception of the teacher's job. The more frequent feeling that teaching is a daily challenge tallies with the greater feeling of uncertainty already mentioned.

On the whole, the above findings are similar within each country, whatever the zone. However, in French rural areas (Zone 1), considerably fewer teachers said that teaching is a hard job. This can be explained by the working conditions: integration within the local community, type of pupils and above all class size, French rural schools having by far the smallest classes (Chapter 5). Also, it is in the inner city (Zone 3) where the smallest proportion of teachers agreed that teaching is a 'vocation' (only 57 per cent agree) or 'is a way of giving meaning to my life' (54 per cent compared with an average of 68 per cent for the French cohort as a whole, and 72 per cent for the English cohort).

Table 7.2   *Teachers' conceptions of their role (factor analysis)*

Statements	Loading	
	French	English
Idealism		
1. It is a vocation	0.79	0.82
5. It is a way of giving meaning to my life	0.71	0.64
4. It is about the daily pleasure of contact with children	0.55	0.57
2. It is a way of earning one's living like		
any other	−0.81	−0.72
Realism		
6. It is a very hard job	0.81	0.83
7. It is to be daily disillusioned	0.82	0.76
8. It is to do a job little valued by society	0.60	0.49
Social possibilities		
3. It is adventure in collective creation with my colleagues	0.75	0.45
9. It gives one the possibility of interesting social relationships	0.48	0.76
10. It is being isolated in one's work	−0.59	−0.65

Again, in the French inner city, there are almost twice as many teachers who feel that teaching 'is a means of earning a living like any other'. We shall return later to an explanation of these differences between inner-city teachers and teachers in other zones. As far as the English cohort is concerned, there are no significant differences between zones. English teachers on the whole share similar views of teaching regardless of the social location of the school in which they work.

'Idealism', 'realism' and 'social integration'

When a factor analysis was carried out on the data, three dimensions emerged which appeared to underlie teachers' conception of their work. These were: 'idealism', 'realism' and 'social integration'. 'Idealism' is a factor composed of a group of statements covering teaching as a 'vocation', 'giving meaning to life' and 'the pleasure of contact with children'. The same group of teachers who responded positively to these responded negatively to the statement that teaching is 'simply a means of earning a living'. 'Realism' is the factor made up of positive responses to the statements that teaching is 'a daily challenge', 'a very hard job' and 'a job little valued by society'. Finally we gave the name 'social integration' to the factor composed of the two statements that teaching is 'collaboration with colleagues' and 'gives interesting social relationships'. The group of teachers who responded positively to these also responded negatively to the statement that teaching is 'being isolated in my work'. These three dimensions enable us to sum-marize the responses to question 27. They also form the basis for a more detailed analysis of the comparisons discussed above (Table 7.2).

Explanation of factor analysis

The particular type of factorial analysis used (varimax rotation using the three most significant factors) reveals an identical structure, which is also a simple structure, for both cohorts. The three factors, which for both cohorts account for more than 50 per

Table 7.3   *Idealism: influence of gender and age of teacher*

Population		Sex		Age			30–45 yrs		>45 yrs	
		M	F	<30	30–45	>45	M	F	M	F
France	M*	15.9	17.9	14.6	17.1	18.7	15.8	17.7	17.6	19.0
	SD*	4.4	4.3	4.0	4.3	4.1	4.5	4.1	3.9	4.1
	No.	117	242	59	175	122	48	126	33	89
England	M*	16.4	17.1	16.6	16.5	17.3	16.2	16.9	16.7	17.7
	SD*	3.8	3.7	3.5	3.9	3.6	3.9	3.8	3.6	3.6
	No.	133	196	35	188	107	84	103	38	69

*M, mean; SD, standard deviation.

cent of the total variance, are easy to interpret. The first factor has a strong positive loading for question 1 (vocation) (0.79 and 0.82), question 5 (meaning to my life) (0.71 and 0.64), question 4 (contact with children) (0.55 and 0.57), and a negative loading for question 2 (a means of earning a living like any other) (-0.81 and -0.72). The second factor has a strong loading for the variables 'a very hard job' (0.81 and 0.82), 'a daily challenge' (0.82 and 0.76) and 'a job which is little valued by society' (0.60 and 0.49). Finally, the most highly loaded questions for the third factor are, on the positive side, question 3 ('collaboration in a creative endeavour with my colleagues') (0.75 and 0.45) and question 9 ('the chance of interesting social relationships') (0.48 and 0.76), and on the negative side question 10 ('being isolated in my work') (-0.59 and -0.65).

Three general conclusions can be drawn from Table 7.2 and from further analysis of zone differences in factor scores. First of all, despite the 'idealism' which is a strong characteristic of both groups of teachers' concept of their work, 'realism' is the major element for both groups of teachers. Although the teacher's job is perceived as depending on a sense of vocation, and carrying a high degree of personal satisfaction through the contact with children, it is also seen first and foremost as a hard job which is little valued by society. This is true in both countries. Secondly, the country of origin does not affect the scores relating to the dimensions 'idealism' and 'realism'. This is not the case, however, for 'social integration'. Whatever the zone, the scores for 'social integration' are much higher for the English cohort (mean score = 15.9) than for the French cohort (mean score = 12.9). This difference, the value of which is almost as high as a standard deviation, is very important. It would appear that French teachers feel a lack of social support in comparison with the English. Thirdly, whilst English teachers' scores are similar regardless of the social location of their schools, there is a significant difference between teachers in the inner city in France and teachers in more advantaged areas as far as the dimension of 'idealism' is concerned. It appears that teachers in the French inner city have a considerably less idealized conception of their job than their colleagues from the other zones.

Since we have already noted (Chapter 4) that the French inner city has a much higher proportion of male teachers, and of young teachers, than the other zones, it is necessary to ask whether the lesser idealism of inner-city teachers can be explained by these two characteristics. On this question, Table 7.3 shows that there is indeed for both countries, though considerably more so for the French cohort, a correlation between age and sex, and the scores for the dimension 'idealism', the influence of each factor remaining when the other is held constant. 'Idealism' increases with age, and is more noticeable for women teachers. But the combined influence of age and sex cannot explain alone the lesser degree of 'idealism' for inner-city teachers. Even when age and sex have the same values, the scores for 'idealism' are still less for those teachers. The children and families with whom they work do not lead French inner-city teachers to declare their job to be harder, but the feeling that teaching is a vocation is less common here, and these teachers are more cynical about the affective rewards to be reaped from their job. Clearly this is not the case among inner-city teachers in England.

SUMMARY AND CONCLUSIONS

The two kinds of data analysed in this chapter show that both French and English teachers felt that theirs is a hard job, little valued by society, which has as its main redeeming feature the contact with children. The idea that teaching is a vocation, with the degree of idealism that this entails, is therefore very much alive. This is probably the case for many social professions influenced historically by an altruistic and humanitarian ideology.

It is not surprising that in France this idealism should be more of a feature for women teachers, and should increase with age. The low salaries and the prevailing notion that primary school teaching is a woman's job do not make the profession attractive to men, and those men who do choose the profession might well do so because of circumstance rather than because of a vocation. The fact that idealism increases with age might be a peculiarity of that particular generation of teachers. It is possible that those teachers who are over the age of 45 joined the profession at a time when the notion of teaching as a vocation was rather more common than it is now. But this increase might also be due to the lack of incentive provided by low salaries and a job little valued by society. French teachers who want to carry on believing in their job have therefore no alternative but, year after year, to rely on an idealization of their job, and the feeling of personal satisfaction that goes along with this. By contrast, in England, there is a greater possibility of career progression through becoming a deputy head, then a head, particularly the head of a large school.

We also argued that both English and French teachers see their professional responsibilities strongly in terms of accountability regarding objectives to be reached. But the commitment and conscientiousness expressed by both groups relate to two different conceptions of the nature of teachers' work, the first one being broad or 'extended' (and more characteristic of the English teachers), the second one being narrow, or 'restricted' (and more characteristic of the French teachers).

The differences noted above correspond closely to the differences mentioned in Chapter 6 in the area of teaching practice. The more flexible practices of the English teacher – in the areas of the objectives to be reached in class, extracurricular activities, collaboration with parents and colleagues – correspond to a conception of the teacher's role which sees teachers as integrated within the community of the school, a community which shares their preoccupations and responsibilities. It is this 'culture of collaboration' (Nias *et al.*, 1989) within the English primary school which leads English teachers to feel far more strongly than their French counterparts that their job gives the chance of interesting social relationships. This also explains why, even though they feel the job is little valued by society, their view of the social value of the job is less pessimistic.

On the other hand, the considerably less flexible and less collaborative practices of the French teachers correspond to a conception of the teacher as a relatively isolated worker, whose world revolves around the classroom, and who is mostly preoccupied with the acquisition of narrow educational objectives. This leads to a more personalized conception of professional responsibility, with a greater need for certainty, and a clear definition of the job and its objectives. There is in fact a large degree of coherence between teaching practices and the aspects covered in our study. It is as if the different conditions of work and functioning of the school as an institution, which are characteristic of the two educational systems, lead the teachers to perceive their role in a way which legitimizes their practices.

Apart from this striking general difference in pedagogical models between the two countries, there is a second difference which relates to the variation observed within each country. There are far more marked differences between teachers working in different socio-economic zones in France than there are in England. This is true particularly of one of the dimensions which make up the conception of the teacher's role: 'idealism'. For the French teachers the effects of age and sex on this dimension are the most marked. There is an obvious parallel here with the effects (mentioned in Chapter 5) of these same variables on the careers of the teachers. As we saw earlier, in France being a woman and/or being a more experienced teacher make it more likely that a teacher will be nominated to posts in areas which offer much sought-after living and teaching conditions. Since the teachers from those areas are satisfied with their working and living conditions, they tend to idealize their job more than their colleagues who teach in other areas. Such an explanation is all the more likely since the analyses carried out showed that the degree of idealism varied according to the location of the school in France, the inner-city schools being those where the degree of idealism was lowest.

No such phenomenon is observed in England. The difference between the two countries can be explained partly by the existence of differences mentioned elsewhere (Chapters 3 and 5) in the appointment systems. The greater freedom experienced by English teachers in the search for a post may allow for greater job satisfaction, since the career of French teachers is constrained by a body of administrative regulations. The location of the schools is less likely to affect the idealism of the English teachers, since it is the teacher who voluntarily chooses to apply for a specific post at a specific school. Moreover, it is likely that the freedom given to English schools and teachers in the adjustment of curriculum and teaching methods is a contributing factor in the reinforcement of self-motivation. This may be another reason for the lack of influence of the location of schools on the idealism of the English teachers. If, as Nias (1989) argues, English teachers' professional satisfaction depends closely upon their ability to move between schools until they find one where the ethos matches their own educational values, it is not surprising that the location of the school does not appear to be significant. French teachers, by contrast, typically must wait a good many years to achieve a post in their desired school and it is arguably for this reason that the degree of idealism so closely reflects the school location.

Chapter 8

The Goals of Teaching

In this chapter we investigate what outcomes the teachers hope to achieve through their teaching. Our purpose was first of all to assess, through an open-ended question, the main long-term educational outcomes sought by the teachers. They were then asked, through a series of fixed-response questions, to evaluate the degree of responsibility they felt regarding each one of the objectives given in a standardized list. Comparisons of teachers' views in the four different socio-economic zones are also presented.

SHORT-TERM, MEDIUM-TERM AND LONG-TERM EDUCATIONAL GOALS

Teachers were invited to respond to the following question:

> 'Your work as a teacher can have short-term, medium-term and long-term outcomes. What are likely to be the most important outcomes of your own teaching for your pupils? (a) In the short term, i.e. in the course of this school year? (b) In the medium term, i.e. as they complete compulsory schooling? (c) In the long term, i.e. when your pupils have become adults?

The question presupposes that teachers' objectives are not merely short-term, and that they consider teaching outcomes which have repercussions for the future lives of their pupils. This presupposition showed itself to be close to reality for the bulk of the English cohort, where 99 per cent of the replies referred to short-term outcomes, 96 per cent to medium-term outcomes, and 98 per cent to long-term outcomes. This was not the case for the French cohort. Whilst a very high percentage of replies referred to short-term outcomes (92 per cent), only 82 per cent and 81 per cent referred respectively to medium-term and to long-term outcomes. Moreover, 18 per cent of the replies which referred to long-term outcomes said that there is no such outcome, or that the teachers felt no responsibility in this area (see Table 8.2). In other words, two French teachers in every ten gave no important and durable medium-term outcomes for their teaching; and more than three teachers in every ten gave no long-term outcomes. We shall attempt to find some explanation for this later on.

Table 8.1   *Short-term and medium-term outcomes of teaching: percentage of teachers mentioning each category*

Teaching objectives	Short-term		Medium-term	
	France	England	France	England
Basic skills (reading, writing, arithmetic)	65.0	28.8	30.7	11.7
Other academic knowledge	40.2	14.7	18.2	4.0
Desire to learn and good study habits	32.3	39.6	46.7	38.1
Intellectual development	13.8	39.0	18.9	19.7
Socialization	16.4	20.4	14.0	16.6
Development of the personality	13.4	26.8	8.0	20.1
Total development	6.3	19.1	3.1	10.0
Physical development	1.6	1.0	0.9	0.0
Understanding of the world	1.6	1.0	2.2	2.4
Civic education	0.4	0.0	0.9	1.8
Moral education	0.8	0.4	1.8	1.4
Aesthetic/artistic education	0.0	1.1	0.4	1.4
Preparation for leisure	0.0	0.7	0.0	2.0
Preparation for the future	1.2	16.7	15.5	34.6

Note: Since teachers could mention more than one category, percentages equal more than 100.

Short-term and medium-term educational outcomes

All of the themes present in the replies were sorted out between the 14 categories in Table 8.1. First of all, it was extremely rare for both English and French teachers to say that their teaching would be likely to have a noticeable outcome on the physical, civic, moral or aesthetic development of children, or for their preparation for leisure and their general understanding of the world. Rather, the most common outcomes anticipated were the acquisition of knowledge, the formation of the intellect and of the mind, the desire to learn, socialization and the growth of the individual. This last theme was analysed as two different categories, 'growth of the individual' and 'overall development', the former referring to characteristics such as 'sensitivity', 'self-esteem', 'self-confidence' and 'emotional development', and the latter to the growth of the whole individual, covering all aspects of the personality.

The differences that can be observed in Table 8.1 appear to reflect two different conceptions of the teacher's role. The French conception leads the teacher to see the child more as a 'pupil', where the emphasis tends to be on the 'immediate' product (academic results) to be achieved. The English conception, on the other hand, leads the teacher to see the child more as a 'person', with an emphasis on processes (cognitive attitudes) to be developed.

There was a very substantial difference between the French and the English teachers in the area of knowledge to be acquired at school, especially basic skills (writing, arithmetic), as well as other academic subjects. These are the short-term outcomes that appeared most often for the French sample, with 65 per cent of teachers mentioning basic skills and 40 per cent mentioning the acquisition of knowledge in the other subjects. This was not the case for the English cohort. These outcomes were mentioned only by 29 per cent and 15 per cent respectively of the teachers. When it came to medium-term objectives, academic knowledge in a subject area was mentioned less often, but the differences between teachers in the two countries was even more marked: basic skills were still mentioned by 31 per cent and other subjects by 18 per cent of the French teachers, as opposed to only 12 per cent and 4 per cent respectively of the English teachers.

On the other hand, the English teachers mentioned more often than their French colleagues important outcomes regarding the growth of the individual, and the overall growth of the child. This was true for both short-term outcomes and for medium-term outcomes, as Tables 8.1 and 8.2 indicate.

The English teachers also mentioned more frequently than their French counterparts (39 per cent compared with 14 per cent) important short-term outcomes involving intellectual development, although, interestingly, this difference was no longer present regarding medium-term outcomes. This may be because there is evidence to suggest that the terms embrace different emphases for the two groups. The French teachers mentioned more frequently 'intellectual development' and 'a critical mind', whilst the English teachers were more likely to talk of developing 'intellectual curiosity' or 'an independent attitude to the management of their own learning situations'. In one case, the emphasis is on outcomes relating to the training of the mind, in the other on inculcating in children the desire and ability to acquire new knowledge.

Similar differences of emphasis were found regarding teaching children working habits and inculcating the desire to learn. More than a third of the teachers from both cohorts said that these outcomes are important, whether short-term or medium-term, the figures being even higher for the French cohort (47 per cent compared with 38 per cent) when talking of medium-term outcomes. But the French teachers tended to talk of 'a liking for work well done' or for 'a taste for effort and perseverance', whilst their English counterparts again emphasized the development of 'the intellectual curiosity' of the children and of 'a newly awakened interest in subjects they have a flair for'.

Similarly, socialization – the development of children's social attitudes and behaviour – is of moderate importance as a goal to teachers in both countries. Roughly one teacher in every five mentioned these, whether as short-term or as medium-term outcomes. But the French teachers more often added moral connotations, through the use of expressions like 'a respect for the other members of the group', 'good habits (tidiness, unaffectedness, good behaviour, punctuality, politeness)', 'social responsibility', whilst the English teachers remained in the area of relationships, using expressions such as 'learning to form good relationships with each other', 'to become more aware and able to relate to others'.

All of the differences mentioned above confirm and add to the general trends discussed in the previous chapter. There is on the French side the overriding influence of a conception of the teacher's role which favours outcomes such as the acquisition of academic knowledge and the development of a love for work and of intellectual and moral rigour. For the English side, on the other hand, the overriding influence is that of a more 'open' conception which puts emphasis on the development of the individual and on the ability to function independently within a group where the child has to learn to establish good relationships. It is not surprising therefore that, since they concentrate more on the individual as a whole than on the child as pupil, the replies of the English teachers should mention more frequently as an outcome of their teaching a preparation for life (17 per cent mentioned this as a short-term outcome as opposed to 1 per cent for the French cohort, and 35 per cent as a medium-term outcome as opposed to 16 per cent for the French cohort). This difference tallies entirely with what was said at the beginning of this chapter, and also reveals a further difference in the way teachers feel about the projection into the future of their professional responsibility. We shall return to this theme later.

Long-term educational outcomes

It is striking that only two-thirds of the French teachers (66 per cent) said that they have a long-term influence on children whilst most of the English teachers felt this (92 per cent). A number of authors (e.g. Jackson, 1968; Hargreaves, 1984) have already noted that teachers do not systematically declare long-term objectives when they talk of their professional responsibility. Our data suggest that this can be the result of two different attitudes. Either their reply is something like 'I am not sure my teaching has long-term outcomes' (an English teacher); it is reasonable to think in this case that teachers assume that pupils will be exposed to many other influences, and that they are not at all certain that their influence will still have some effect when the pupils have become adults. Or the reply follows the model, 'I certainly hope that my teaching has no long-term outcomes! To imagine anything else suggests that one wants to mould individuals to fit a certain social category, rather than that one wants to help them develop their own individual capabilities' (a French teacher). In this case, the underlying assumption is of an ethical nature. It is reasonable to assume that it is in the name of individual freedom that teachers feel they cannot possibly exercise an influence of some importance other than in the area of immediate scholastic pursuits.

The difference which appears between the two cohorts can probably be explained by this distinction between the 'realistic' and the 'ethical' view. It is also likely that the latter reason is the more important, since the French republican ideology of the school detached from the Church, with its strong commitment to neutrality, implies that the teacher's influence on future adults should be confined to academic matters. This might also explain why some French teachers say that this question does not concern them.

When asked about the likely long-term effects of their teaching, the teachers' replies reflected three main types of preoccupation. These concern: (a) the training of the citizen, the development of reason, of thinking and of the critical mind; (b) the emotions, and their place within the development of the individual; and (c) social roles and responsibilities. The first type of outcome occurred slightly more frequently for the French cohort, particularly in the area of civics and the training of the future citizen (36 per cent compared with 30 per cent), whilst the other two types of outcomes come up much more frequently for the English cohort (Table 8.2). In fact, three times as many English teachers mentioned good relationships with others (26 per cent compared with 8 per cent) and a happy personality (13 per cent compared with 5 per cent). Also, more English teachers mentioned as an important outcome of their teaching a contribution towards the production of adults who are 'well-balanced' (22 per cent compared with 12 per cent), 'mature' (15 per cent compared with 11 per cent), 'fully developed' (10 per cent compared with 3 per cent), 'who enjoy learning' (8 per cent compared with 5 per cent). Finally, more English teachers (although some of the figures are low) felt that an important outcome of their teaching is successful entry and integration of the adult into the world of work (15 per cent compared with 8 per cent), preparation for parenthood (4 per cent compared with 2 per cent) and the production of environmentally responsible adults (3 per cent compared with 1 per cent). All of these differences followed the same pattern as the differences regarding short- and medium-term outcomes.

Whether the outcomes considered are short, medium or long-term, the differences between zones were on the whole negligible. It is only in relation to those teachers drawn from the French inner-city zone that a number of interesting features must be noted. We shall comment on these at the end of the chapter, together with the differences which came from the replies to the closed questions.

Table 8.2   *Long-term outcomes of teaching: percentage of teachers mentioning each category*

Teaching objectives	France	England
Training of good citizens	36.3	29.5
Development of reason and critical thinking	22.9	18.6
Development of well-balanced adults	11.7	22.3
Development of good relationships with others	8.1	25.8
Development into mature adults	10.8	15.0
Influence on future careers	7.6	14.5
Development of a joy in living	4.5	12.5
That children should have happy memories of school	9.0	7.3
Development of a pleasure in learning	4.9	8.0
Development of well-rounded adults	2.7	10.1
Preparation for parenthood	1.8	4.8
Development of creative adults	1.3	4.1
Development of environmental awareness	0.8	3.2
Training to be good communicators	2.2	2.0
That children should learn to think of others	0.9	0.7
Long-term outcomes do not concern me	11.7	4.0
My actions do not have long-term effects	6.3	2.1

Note: Since teachers could mention more than one category, percentages could add up to more than 100.

RESPONSIBILITY FOR TEACHING OBJECTIVES

We shall now consider the replies to question 22, which listed 19 objectives and asked: 'In your professional practice, how important is the responsibility you have for the following educational objectives?' The teachers were given the choice of six replies, ranging from 'essential' (5) to 'not important at all' (0).

The status of this question is different from that of the previous open-ended question. The aim was no longer to discover how teachers rank the importance of particular outcomes, but how far they feel they share in the responsibility for promoting those outcomes. It is perfectly plausible for a teacher to feel an important share of responsibility regarding a specific objective whilst at the same time feeling that the actual outcome is not very significant. Also, this question did not involve any differences connected to different time scales. The teachers were merely asked to indicate their share of responsibility regarding outcomes without, for the most part, any indication as to whether these were short-, medium- or long-term. For this reason we should not necessarily expect any direct relationship between the results for this question and those for the previous one. We shall see, however, that there was a large degree of agreement between the two sets of responses.

Figure 8.1 shows that there is a correlation of 0.72 between the French and English ranking of objectives for which teachers feel responsible. Not surprisingly both English and French teachers felt they have a large share of responsibility (average figures ranging from 4.1 to 4.6) in the area of scholastic learning and the inculcation of a taste for learning. Also, for both cohorts, physical education, artistic/aesthetic education and sex education are the least important objectives.

Despite the relative similarity of the rankings, the replies of the English teachers do show a greater concern for educational objectives other than the purely academic ones. For instance, they feel a much higher degree of responsibility for sex education, artistic/aesthetic education, training of the future citizen, moral education, behaviour in class and a concern that 'children should be kept constructively engaged.' Here again, the English teachers' replies are characterized by a wider conception of professional responsibility and of the aims of education.

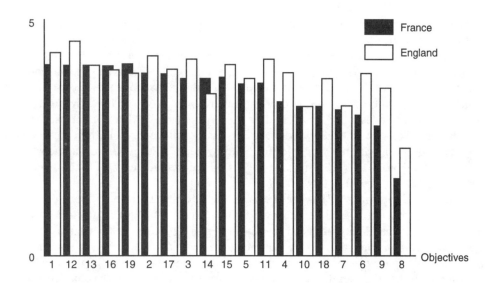

Figure 8.1 The importance ascribed by teachers to their responsibility for various teaching objectives: mean scores of teachers in England and France. 1, Actual instruction/academic work; 12, arouse an interest in learning; 13, that children should enjoy what they are doing; 16, that children see the relevance of what they are doing; 19, helping the child to become mature; 2, development of the child's personality; 17, that pupils should be able to apply their knowledge in the future; 3, training in personal relations; 14, that children should like hard work and effort; 15, that children are kept constructively engaged; 5, development of the intelligence; 11, children's behaviour in class; 4, moral education; 10, health education; 18, that children know how to organize their work; 7, physical education; 6, training of the future citizen; 9, artistic/aesthetic education; 8, sex education

The ranking of objectives based on the amount of responsibility assumed by the teachers is very similar, from one zone to the next, for both cohorts. Although the correlation for the two general rankings is 0.72, the correlation between zones for each national cohort varies between 0.85 and 0.95. Therefore, a much higher degree of similarity exists between the different zones for the same country than there is between the two countries. We may therefore conclude that teachers' sense of their professional responsibility for the various educational objectives listed is most strongly influenced by their involvement in a common national socio-professional culture, rather than any particular set of teaching conditions or pupil characteristics. It is worth noting, however, that the teachers from the French inner city tended to feel a smaller share of responsibility for a number of objectives. There was no such phenomenon for the English cohort.

A principal-components analysis revealed an important general factor informing the responses, which was almost the same for both cohorts, accounting for about a third of the total variance for both cohorts. This means that the main differentiating factor between the teachers from both cohorts is the degree of responsibility that they feel they have.

This general factor, however, does not have the same meaning for both cohorts. If we consider the eight variables which are statistically the most strongly related to this general factor, six relate to academic work and the acquisition of knowledge for the French cohort, whilst this is the case for only two of those variables for the English cohort. On the other hand, only two of those variables in the French data relate to the personal and social development of the individual, whilst this is the case for five of these variables for the English cohort. It is therefore apparent that the basis for the feeling of responsibility is different, as it covers a wider variety of objectives for the English cohort.

This is a reflection of a more open conception of the teacher's role, which includes the personal and social development of the individual, whilst in France the conception of the teacher's role shows a greater concern for purely academic objectives. In the French responses there was thus a correlation of above 0.60 for objectives such as 'arouse an interest in learning', 'that children should like hard work and effort' and 'that children should enjoy what they are doing'. For the French teacher, children must work hard, and this hard work must be a source of enjoyment. This is a characteristic which was isolated by Voluzan (1975) in his analysis of reports written by French regional school inspectors after school visits.

There are no important differences between the different socio-economic zones for this general factor, although the scores are slightly lower for the French inner-city areas. This tallies with the already noted tendency for French teachers in these areas to feel slightly less responsible regarding a number of objectives. The analyses undertaken show that this finding may be associated with the relative youth of those teachers. Certainly it is clear that conditions peculiar to this zone, whether in the characteristics of the children or in those of the teachers, affect the general feeling of responsibility that these teachers have.

SUMMARY AND CONCLUSIONS

When asked to assess their share of responsibility for a number of educational objectives, it is not surprising that teachers should place at the top of the list their responsibility for instruction (academic knowledge, and a desire to learn), and that, by contrast, their responsibility for sex education should be placed at the bottom of the list. The opposite would have been surprising in countries where a major aim of the primary school – as in most other places – is to teach children to read, write and do mathematics.

However, although the teachers from the English cohort felt that they have a large share of responsibility for the pupils' acquisition of basic skills (the three Rs), they did not consider, unlike their French counterparts, that this was the most important outcome of their teaching. And they allocated different degrees of importance to the same outcomes when considering the short-, medium- and long-term.

This means that, although there are trivial similarities between the two cohorts, the replies of the teachers are characterized by two very different conceptions of the teacher's role. We saw that the French conception emphasizes the fact that the child is a pupil, and that it is the teacher's duty to nurture in the child a taste for hard work and the intellectual ability to deal with academic tasks. The English conception on the other hand emphasizes the fact that the child is a person, and that it is the teacher's duty to ensure that the child develops into a social being who can have good personal relations and an interest in things other than the strictly academic. These two conceptions tally entirely with the general tendencies noted in the previous chapter regarding the prevailing conceptions of the nature of the job, and of professional responsibility. The 'restricted' nature of the French conception, which follows from the historical development of a school system characterized by secularism and independence from the Church, probably explains why many teachers felt reluctant to accept that they could or should have a strong influence on the shaping of their pupils into adults. On the other hand, the broader English conception, characterized by a concern for the social integration of the individual, tends to lead teachers to accept that they can and should have a role to play in the development of long-term outcomes.

We also saw that, for both cohorts, the different teaching conditions to be found in the different zones did not alter significantly the above findings. The teachers from all four zones gave the same ranking to the different areas of responsibility. The rankings are also the same for the outcomes which they felt to be the most important. For both cohorts, the prevailing influence of one national education system and its associated socio-professional values appeared to override the effect of the social conditions which characterized the different zones.

Within this general context of similarities within each of the two countries, the few differences noted are interesting. They are connected with the inner-city zone in France. The French teachers from this zone tended to feel a smaller share of responsibility for a number of objectives: they felt less responsible than their colleagues from other zones when it came to getting the children to like hard work, to keeping them constructively engaged, and to teaching them to organize their work. Similarly, fewer teachers from the French inner city felt that the acquisition of academic knowledge is the most important outcome of their teaching. And yet there was no corresponding feeling that some other outcomes are more important (in the area of social relationships, for instance). It is as if many French inner-city teachers have a fatalistic attitude regarding their pupils. When faced with pupil motivation and performance which is judged to be unsatisfactory, these teachers probably put forward in their defence the social and family background of the children in order to reduce their share of responsibility and hence to exonerate themselves from any potential failure.

Such a tendency to devalue the acquisition of scholastic knowledge was also observed for the teachers of the English inner-city zone, whether in relation to the outcomes of teaching or to the teacher's share of the responsibility. Such teachers did tend, however, to place slightly more emphasis on the personal and social development of the child. What happens here seems to be the reverse of what happens in the French inner city; the teachers who work in disadvantaged areas in England appear to react by feeling a greater sense of responsibility regarding those objectives which are deemed to be particularly important by teachers in England generally. We had already noted at the end of the previous chapter that the inner-city teachers had different attitudes in France and in England. This was true, for instance, where the idealism of the French teachers was concerned, although this was not the case for the English teachers. These differences may well reflect the appointment system peculiar to each country; it will be recalled that in France teachers are frequently appointed to posts in disadvantaged areas when they do not particularly wish to end up there. Such teachers have had little preparation to help them cope with the demands of such posts. In England, by contrast, teachers will typically have chosen such postings. It is clear that such structural differences between the appointments procedure in the two systems are likely to have consequences both for teachers' idealism, and for the degree of responsibility teachers feel when confronted with problems.

Chapter 9

Influences and Constraints on Practice

The data analysed in this chapter relate in a very general fashion to the teachers' views on the influences and constraints which affect their teaching practice. Three types of questions are involved. The first attempts to assess the weight given to various factors which influence teachers' work; the second attempts to assess the amount of freedom and the nature of the constraints which teachers perceive regarding teaching methods and curriculum; the third relates to the nature of the controls which operate on the outcomes of pupil and teacher performance. The justification for these different types of question is that the relationship between the importance of a specific influence and the related constraint which this influence exerts is not necessarily straightforward: a specific influence which is felt to be important is not necessarily felt to be constraining if its existence is felt to be justified (for example, the influence of the pupils), whilst a rather less important influence can be perceived as constraining if it is not perceived as legitimate (for example, national policy impositions). Thus, there is no straightforward relationship between the *strength* of a given influence or constraint and the *degree of control* which that influence exerts.

When presenting our results, we shall emphasize, as for the previous chapters, the comparison between the two countries, and the differences due to the socio-economic location of the schools. The other factors taken into account (age and sex, particularly) will be mentioned only where they exert a significant influence.

INFLUENCES ON TEACHERS' PRACTICE

The teachers were asked to reply to two different sets of questions. In the first set of questions they were asked to estimate on a five-point scale the degree of importance attached to 15 possible influences on their teaching practice (question 17) (Figure 9.1). The question we posed was the following:

'In your work as a teacher, how far do you feel that your teaching practice is influenced by each of the following factors?'

The influences listed included that of pupils and of their parents; colleagues, head-teachers and advisers; the influence of the teacher's own family background, teaching experience, personal reading and independent study, and professional ideology; the effect of initial training, in-service training, other courses of various types including study for a university degree or diploma; membership of a professional association; and participation in extracurricular activities with children. In the second question, teachers were asked to agree or disagree on a five-point scale with ten general statements about teaching (question 25). These statements, which are listed in Figure 9.2, took up again some of the themes outlined above, but they also asked for teachers' views on more general social factors (the role of the State and of government policy, the effect of the social location of the school and of local socio-economic conditions on teaching).

Findings

If we examine first the degree of importance which teachers attach to the 15 possible influences on their teaching practice listed in question 17, two findings of considerable interest emerge. Looking both at the average scores for the two countries (Figure 9.1) and at the average scores by zone, it is clear that whilst there are considerable differences between teachers in the two countries, there is, on the contrary, a very striking agreement between teachers working in different socio-economic zones within the same country.

On a very general level, the teachers from both countries felt that their personal experience, their pupils, their colleagues and their own reading and independent study were four of the five most important influences on their teaching practice. Similarly, the teachers from both countries felt that experience of specialist personal courses and study for a university degree are among the four least important influences on their teaching practice. However, the correlation (Spearman's rho) between the two general rankings is only 0.55, which shows that the similarity is not complete. The English teachers placed considerably more emphasis than their French counterparts on the importance of their professional ideology (mean score $M = 3.1$, as opposed to 1.9), on the influence of their headteacher ($M = 2.6$ compared with $M = 1.9$), and on their participation in extracurricular activities with children ($M = 2.4$ compared with $M = 1.5$).

Conversely, the French teachers placed considerably more emphasis on the importance of the school inspector ($M = 2.3$ compared with $M = 1.4$) and on their participation in in-service training ($M = 2.1$ compared with $M = 1.3$). These differences between the two countries appear regardless of the location of the schools, the large degree of agreement within each country being confirmed by very similar mean scores for each variable from one zone to the next, and by very high correlations between the rankings established from the teachers' answers for each zone. In France, those correlations are all between .90 and .96, and in England between .90 and .99.

Looking at the reactions of the teachers to the ten statements in question 25 relating to the influences on their teaching practices, the results presented in Figure 9.2 are cumulative percentages for the replies 'strongly agree' and 'agree to some extent'. Again, the general data (Figure 9.2) and the breakdown by zone reveal clear differences between the two countries, and a very large degree of agreement for all the teachers of the same country, regardless of the zone. This is confirmed by correlations ranging from .92 to .98 in France, and from .91 to .95 in England, between the rankings of the ten statements according to the percentages of agreement expressed in each zone.

We must stress first of all that this confirms the finding discussed above, that there is a considerable difference between the teachers of the two countries regarding the

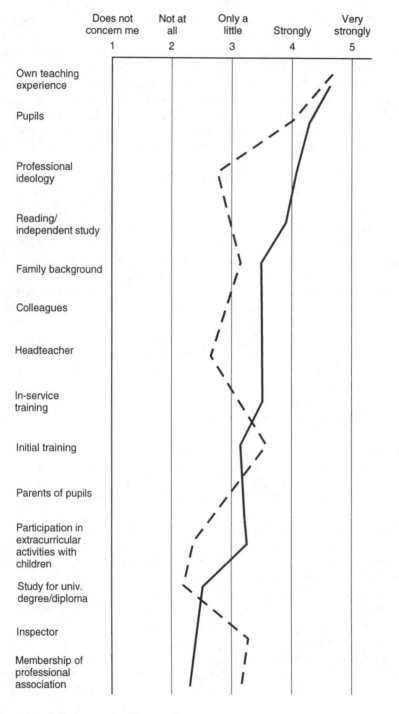

Figure 9.1   Influences on teaching practice

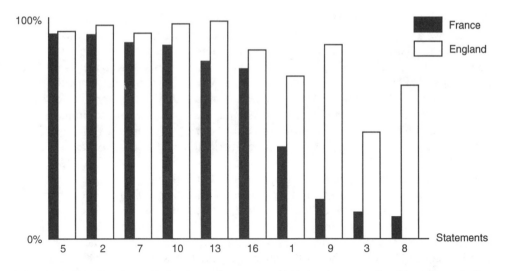

Figure 9.2 Teachers' views of influences and constraints: 5, the teacher must adapt his or her methods to the social composition of the local area; 2, it is up to teachers to decide, on the basis of their professional experience, what is best for the child; 7, teachers' activities in the classroom must take into account the needs and the socio-economic characteristics of the local environment; 10, teachers should be available to discuss personal matters with parents; 13, teachers should be ready to listen to parents' opinions; 16, the teacher must adapt the content of her teaching to the social composition of the local area; 1, parents should have a say in what their children learn at school; 9, what teachers do from day to day should reflect the policy of the head; 3, a teacher's practice should follow the directions laid down by government policy; 8, teachers should adapt their teaching (curriculum and methods) to meet parents' wishes. *Note:* The numbers correspond to the statements in question 25 of the questionnaire (see Appendix 1)

importance attributed to school heads. This is not surprising given the different responsibilities that school heads have in the two countries (see Chapter 3).

The replies relating to the socio-economic characteristics of the local community, however, do introduce fresh information. The majority (and sometimes virtually all) of teachers of both countries said that 'it is up to the teachers to decide, on the basis of their professional experience, what is best for the child' (90 and 96 per cent), agreeing that 'teachers' activities in the classroom must take into account the needs and the socio-economic characteristics of the local community' (87 and 91 per cent agreeing), and that 'the teacher must adapt his or her methods' (92 per cent agreeing in both countries), and even 'the content of his/her teaching' (74 and 83 per cent agreeing) 'to the social composition of the local area'. Similarly, most teachers also said that 'teachers should be available to discuss personal matters with parents' (85 and 97 per cent) and that they 'should be ready to listen to parents' opinions' (78 and 97 per cent).

Most teachers in both countries therefore felt that they must be open to influences and information coming from the local community, i.e. from outside the school. This belief, however, was a little stronger in England than it was in France. This was the case particularly in relation to the need to discuss personal matters with parents, and to listen to their opinions, where respectively 11 and 19 per cent more English teachers than their French counterparts agreed with the statements. We shall see that the difference between the two countries was even more marked when the statements suggest a direct influence on the part of the family.

The fact is that none of the above statements takes into consideration the way in which these influences or external information apply. This is not so for the two statements where the teachers were asked to agree or disagree with the view that parents should have a direct influence. Both in France and in England the proportion of agreement for these two statements was markedly less than for the previous ones. This was, however, less so for the English cohort, where the majority still agreed with both statements, whilst for the French cohort the majority – and in some cases the overwhelming majority – of teachers disagreed. Only 40 per cent of the French teachers (as opposed to 71 per cent of the English teachers) agreed that parents 'should have a say in what their children learn at school', and only 7 per cent (as opposed to 67 per cent) felt that 'teachers should adapt their teaching (curriculum and methods) to meet parents' wishes.'

In other words, in both countries teachers feel that it is important to be receptive to families, whether it is listening to their opinions, or lending a sympathetic ear to their daily problems. This may be due, at least partly, to the pervasive influence of current views in France as well as in England that the teacher's role should include a sympathetic and receptive attitude towards families. However, although French teachers are willing to adopt such an attitude, they still wish to have the last word! They feel that it is up to them entirely to decide how to handle the pressures they are faced with, and what to make of the needs expressed, as they feel they have the sole responsibility for the practical consequences of these pressures and needs on their teaching. The English attitude is very different. Parents are felt by a significant proportion of teachers to have a legitimate part to play in the choice of teaching objectives and adjustment of teaching methods. English teachers' 'open' or 'extended' conception of the teacher's role and responsibilities leads to a recognition that parents are justified in making their own contribution, whilst the 'narrow' or 'restricted' conception which is characteristic of French teachers leads to a view of such contributions as interfering.

To test still further the impression reported above, factor analysis was used to investigate the underlying attitudinal structures of the two groups. Two factor analyses were performed: one for the French sample, and one for the English. In both analyses the three most important factors were identified. Statements with component loadings of greater than .40 were used to interpret the underlying dimensions (Table 9.1).

For the French cohort, the first dimension is arranged around a group of statements which relate to the influence of training: linking 'experience of specialist personal courses' (.77), 'participation in in-service training' (.58) and 'initial training' (.46), which are all concerned directly with training, with 'extracurricular activities with children' (.71) and 'membership of a professional association' (.47), both of which may involve professional development and learning-related activities. The second dimension can be interpreted as being to do with the school itself, since it includes the teacher herself – 'my own reading/independent study' (.63), 'personal teaching experience' (.55) – and the other persons involved in the running of the school, since the loadings for 'school inspector', 'headteacher' and 'colleagues at work' are .54. The third dimension is essentially to do with influences from outside the school, since the loading is .70 for 'family background', .61 for 'parents', .56 for 'pupils', and .63 for 'professional ideology'.

As for the English cohort, there is also a first dimension relating to training which covers very much the same areas as the corresponding dimension for the French cohort. Out of the five items which have a loading exceeding .40, four are identical with the French analysis 'experience of specialist personal courses' (.67), 'initial training' (.62), 'participation in in-service training' (.58) and 'membership of a professional association' (.47). The two other dimensions, however, are noticeably different. The second dimen-

Table 9.1 *Influences on teaching practice*

France		England	
Variables	Loading	Variables	Loading
First factor			
Training in personal relationships	0.77	Training in personal relationships	0.67
Participation in school-based activities	0.71	Initial training	0.62
Involvement in teaching movement	0.68	Ideology	0.60
Participation in courses	0.58	Participation in courses	0.58
Initial training	0.46	Involvement in teaching movement	0.47
Second factor			
Personal reading	0.63	Colleagues	0.68
Personal experience	0.55	Headteacher	0.67
Inspector	0.54	Inspector	0.56
Headteacher	0.54	Parents of pupils	0.48
Colleagues	0.54		
Third factor			
Influence of own family	0.70	Personal experience	0.67
Ideology	0.63	Pupils	0.60
Parents of pupils	0.61	Personal reading	0.41
Pupils	0.56		

sion groups together the influence of the other persons involved in the running of the school with that of parents, with the following loadings: 'colleagues' (.68), 'headteacher' (.67), 'school inspector' (.56) and parents (.48). The third dimension groups together personal influences with the influence of pupils, with the following loadings: 'personal teaching experience' (.67), 'pupils' (.60) and 'own reading/ independent study' (.41).

There is therefore no clear demarcation for the English cohort between the influence of those involved in the running of the school (the teacher herself, and the other persons involved) and the people who have a direct interest in the school (parents and pupils). This would seem to be indicative of two different conceptions: the first one, in the case of the French cohort, tending to dissociate those two types of influence; the second, in the case of the English cohort, tending to link them together.

Not surprisingly, because of the large degree of similarity already noted between the answers for the different zones for both countries, the particular location of the schools does not have any systematic effect on the results of the three dimensions. This is also the case for differences in the age and sex of the teachers concerned.

Margin of freedom

Teachers were asked how much freedom they felt in terms of both choice of teaching content and teaching methods. In both cases (content and teaching methods), the first question aimed to elicit a general judgement using a five-point scale ('very little freedom or no freedom at all' to 'complete freedom'). The next three questions were open-ended questions: 'For what aspects of your curriculum do you feel you have the greatest freedom of choice?' (Q. 19.b), 'the least freedom of choice?' (Q. 19.c), and 'What are the major constraints which determine for you the content of your teaching?' (Q.19.d). The questions relating to the teaching methods were identical: 'In what aspects do you have the greatest freedom?' (Q. 20.b), 'the least freedom?' (Q. 20.c) and 'What are the major constraints which determine for you your teaching methods?' (Q. 20.d).

We shall first of all look at what the teachers said about the major constraints which affect their teaching before looking at what they said concerning the amount of freedom they perceive themselves as having. The open-ended questions were phrased in such a way that a number of answers were possible. The percentages quoted later can therefore exceed 100 per cent.

Major constraints

The question relating to teaching methods (Q. 20.4) produced a high non-response rate (25 per cent for the French cohort, and 21 per cent for the English cohort). These blanks are difficult to interpret. It may be that many teachers found it difficult to express clear-cut ideas about the major constraints affecting their teaching methods, whilst the major constraints affecting the curriculum seemed much more obvious, particularly for French teachers.

The major constraints which emerge most often in relation to curriculum content (Figure 9.2) are those which refer to the practicalities of the system (programmes of study and physical conditions). This is true for both cohorts, although more so for the French cohort (88 per cent of all teachers, as opposed to 65 per cent). Moreover, when those constraints are mentioned, it is not in the same terms. The vast majority of French teachers (82 per cent) mentioned the programmes of study, but very few mentioned the physical conditions (6 per cent). Considerably fewer English teachers mentioned pro-gtammes of study (32 per cent), and many more mentioned the physical conditions (large classes, lack of money, etc.) (33 per cent). The pattern is similar for the major constraints which affect teaching methods: the English teachers mentioned physical conditions much more often, and the French teachers mentioned the programmes of study much more often. Of course, at the time of our study, a national curriculum had not yet been implemented in English schools, and more recent research suggests that English teachers' perceptions of freedom in choice of content (although not teaching methods) are beginning to alter (Osborn and Pollard, 1990; Pollard *et al.*, 1994).

At the time of the study, then, the constraints which English teachers perceived as emanating from the school system appeared to be rather less heavy than for French teachers, whose constraints originated almost exclusively from the central authority, and were applied through the implementation of a national curriculum. For the English teachers, on the other hand, the constraints originated from the teachers' own schools and from the people who were directly above them within those schools, rather than from the curriculum or programmes of study. It is clear, of course, that not every English school was entirely free to do whatever it wished, and that a number of social constraints operated through various channels. Even though in every school the teachers were involved in the drawing up of programmes of study (see Chapter 3), there existed a number of pressures which tended to have a levelling effect (textbooks available, exter-nally defined criteria and standards), and which restricted the amount of freedom that teachers actually had. Thus only one in three English teachers as opposed to more than two in three French teachers felt that programmes of study were a major constraint on the content of their teaching. By contrast, the emphasis that many of the English teachers placed on the physical conditions of teaching suggests that they felt that the

Table 9.2   *Constraints on teaching*

Constraint	France (%)	England (%)
Curriculum directives	82.0	32.0
Material resources	5.5	33.3
Pupils	30.1	40.9
Outside influences	8.9	13.9
Myself (the teacher)	5.8	25.2
Colleagues	3.8	11.0

freedom they had in designing the curriculum could be even greater if they had at their disposal the appropriate means. In a system which allows for a certain amount of freedom for the teachers, a tailoring of the curriculum to suit the needs of individuals pupil depends, among other things, on physical conditions such as class size and teaching materials available.

The major constraints which relate to the pupils (levels of attainment, behaviour and various other characteristics) come in only second place, after the constraints relating to the school system. The slightly higher frequency of these constraints for the English cohort (41 per cent compared with 30 per cent) can be explained, first of all, because class size is markedly bigger in England (see Chapter 3), a fact which could make the teacher's task rather more onerous where pupils with difficulties are concerned. On the other hand, the degree of freedom which the English teachers have in the choice of curriculum means that the specific abilities of the pupils can be taken into account when choosing appropriate teaching contents. It is not surprising either that characteristics which relate to the pupils themselves crop up more frequently in the school located in working-class areas (Zones 2 and 3) as one of the major constraints. It is in these schools that the level of attainment of the pupils is perceived by teachers to be lower (see Chapter 6). In France, however, those constraints are more frequently mentioned in the inner-city areas (Zone 3), whilst in England it is in Zone 2 (average working-class) that they are slightly more frequently mentioned.

The last three categories of Table 9.2 (the teacher herself, outside influences and colleagues) occur less frequently than the first three, and are all mentioned more often by the English cohort. The difference is particularly marked for the major constraints which relate to the teacher's own characteristics and abilities (25 per cent compared with 6 per cent). But there is still a fairly clear difference between the two cohorts in relation to outside influences as a constraint (14 per cent in England, as opposed to 9 per cent in France) and to colleagues (11 per cent in England as opposed to 4 per cent in France).

The greater constraint emanating from outside influences and from colleagues which is perceived by teachers in England can be explained by the common practice of collaboration with other teachers and the sense of partnership with parents (described earlier) as well as by the broader conception of the teacher's role.

The fact that one English teacher in every four should see her own characteristics and abilities as one of the major constraints affecting her teaching (both in relation to curriculum and to teaching methods) can also be explained in a similar way. It is true that the implementation of compulsory national objectives is felt to be particularly constraining by French teachers, who feel responsible for fulfilling the contract between themselves and their schools. But this contractual responsibility, which implies that the initiative rests with someone else, also means that teachers have no reason to feel that they themselves are limiting what might be achieved in their teaching. The school and the National Curriculum protect and reassure teachers; they could therefore remain

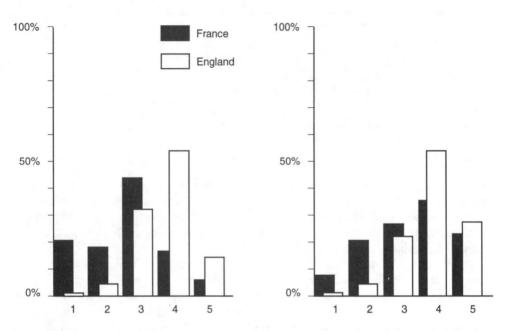

Figure 9.3 Major constraints affecting (a) teaching content and (b) teaching methods: 1, very little freedom or no freedom at all; 2, a little freedom; 3, considerable freedom; 4, a great deal of freedom, 5, complete freedom

relatively more confident about their achievements than their English counterparts.

It is because English teachers were directly involved in the drawing up of aims and objectives – faced with often contradictory demands on the part of parents, children, headteachers and the authorities, and living through those contradictions (Poppleton, 1986) and paradoxes (Nias, 1986) in a very intense fashion – that they more often felt that they themselves were to blame since they had the inner conviction that so much depended on their own actions and decisions. As one teacher put it: 'I take it as a fundamental rule of thumb that I should know I am trying to do something that is impossible to achieve (and so should try not to get disheartened) but these things are so desirable to achieve that you keep trying.'

The burden of responsibility that is placed upon English teachers generates uncertainty, conflict and tension (Hoyle, 1980), and leads them to more frequent feelings of self-doubt and guilt. Another English teacher expressed this in striking terms when describing the teacher's influence on the shaping of the children's lives:

> This responsibility is awesome. No teacher can ever discharge it adequately, so we all carry a burden of guilt that we do not do better. We have to learn to accept this; to acknowledge that we cannot achieve all that children deserve, and set our own level of what each of us, individually, may hope to achieve. In other words, what is the most I can reasonably do, given my limitations of abilities and resources, for any particular child?

Perceptions of freedom

What the teachers say about the degree of freedom they possess generally corresponds entirely with what we have just seen concerning the major constraints which affect their teaching, as Figure 9.3 shows.

On the whole, regardless of the country and zone, the degree of autonomy that the teachers said they have is greater in the area of teaching methods than it is in the area of teaching content. The difference, however, is much greater for the French cohort; the mean percentage of French teachers who felt they have a great deal of freedom or complete freedom was 54 per cent for teaching methods, and only 20 per cent for teaching content. For the English cohort, these percentages were, respectively, 77 per cent and 64 per cent. In all respect, the English teachers perceived themselves as having considerably greater autonomy than their French counterparts. The difference is in fact spectacular in the area of curriculum, where 64 per cent of the English teachers on average said they had 'complete freedom' or 'a great deal of freedom', as opposed to 19 per cent for the French teachers. As for teaching methods, the corresponding figures are 77 per cent and 54 per cent.

The location of the schools does not have a very obvious systematic effect. The only noticeable difference is a very slight tendency for the teachers from affluent middle-class areas (Zone 4) to say more frequently that they have a great deal of freedom as regards both the choice of curriculum and teaching methods, whilst the reverse can be noticed for the English cohort, at least for the curriculum. This difference between the two countries can probably be explained fairly easily. The nature of the school population (children from a privileged background) and the higher level of attainment of the pupils in middle-class areas (compared with Chapter 6) gives the French teachers a greater degree of freedom. Since their pupils acquire fairly easily the compulsory syllabus (teaching content), the teachers feel free to go one step further than the syllabus, and/or to include extra topics. And it is for the same reason that they vary more readily their teaching methods, since their pupils are felt to have a certain degree of adaptability to different techniques. Similarly there is a widespread belief that with less able pupils the emphasis should be placed on the essentials, and that it is most important to adhere rigidly to normal procedures in order not to distract pupils from normal working habits. In England, we saw that teachers are willing to give parents a say in what happens at school. Since middle-class and intellectual parents are seen by teachers to be particularly concerned with their children's schools, it is likely that they affect the choice of teaching content rather more than is the case in the other areas. This may explain why the teachers from the English affluent middle-class areas said slightly less often than the average that they have considerable or a great deal of freedom.

As regards teaching methods, there were considerably more English teachers (37 per cent compared with 19 per cent) who replied that they have great freedom 'in all aspects', and considerably fewer (36 per cent compared with 8 per cent) who replied that they have little. When the English teachers specified the aspects of teaching in which they have the greatest freedom, the two general areas most often identified were classroom organization (33 per cent compared with 20 per cent) and teacher–pupil relations (11 per cent compared with 5 per cent).

In relation to curriculum, both sets of teachers felt they have the greatest freedom in the humanities and arts rather than in the basic skills (80 per cent for the French cohort, and 72 per cent for the English cohort). As for the replies which mentioned a great deal of autonomy in all aspects of the curriculum, they are infrequent for both cohorts, but nevertheless three times as common for the English cohort (12 per cent compared with 4 per cent).

As for the area of the curriculum where there is perceived to be the least freedom of choice, there are considerably fewer French teachers (3 per cent compared with 14 per cent) who mentioned no specific area. In both countries the subjects which were mentioned most are mathematics and language. Eighty-three per cent of the French teachers mentioned mathematics, as opposed to 66 per cent of the English teachers. The difference was even greater for language, where the respective figures are 61 and 20 per cent.

The fact that the humanities and arts subjects should be felt to be the least constraining by the large majority of teachers does not come as a surprise. It is certainly in this area, even in France, that teachers have the greatest freedom of choice because of the particular instructions relating to those subjects. Similarly, there is nothing surprising in the fact that basic subjects like mathematics and language should be felt to be, in both countries, fairly constraining. Whether there is a national curriculum or not, the acquisition of skills in maths, language and reading by the pupils depends on a fairly rigorous approach which may allow less room for manoeuvre. Most teachers see reading, mathematics and language as foundations of the pupils' academic career and do not feel that they can take any liberties in this area. However, despite all this, and this is particularly so for language, these constraints do not seem to be so strong for the English teachers, since they mentioned these subjects less, or considerably less frequently, than their French counterparts when discussing which subjects gave them the least freedom of choice. The only explanation here must be that despite the various constraints present, the greater freedom which applies in the choice of teaching content through the lack of a national curriculum also applies even for the most constraining subjects.

SUMMARY AND CONCLUSIONS

When we examine what teachers say on the whole concerning the influences and constraints on their practice and the areas of freedom, it seems that the differences due to the socio-economic location of the schools within the same country are negligible in comparison with the differences between countries. It appears that the national context of the educational system in each country leads to different conceptions of autonomy and constraint which apply regardless of the sociological characteristics of the different zones, and the working conditions which ensue.

The differences which can be observed between the two populations do not, of course, exclude similarities. Both English and French teachers felt that the school system was the main source of constraint on their freedom, these constraints applying particularly for the foundation subjects, i.e. mathematics and language. This, we argue, is not surprising, since, regardless of the way in which those constraints apply, both school systems are designed to ensure the acquisition of those subjects.

Given this general constraint, both cohorts agreed that they themselves and their immediate environment (pupils and colleagues) play a great part in shaping their teaching practices. In both cases the teachers' conception gives the same weight to close influences which are liable to affect the way they teach.

There are similarities therefore, but there are also differences. We noted first of all that the constraints which emanated from the school system itself were felt to be rather stronger for the French cohort, and that their exact nature was different. In France, these constraints were almost exclusively to do with the programmes of study, whilst in England constraints connected with the content of the curriculum were mentioned three times less often. It follows that English teachers felt they had considerably more freedom than their French counterparts, this difference being even more striking in the area of curriculum than in the area of teaching methods. This greater freedom was felt even in the area of the most constraining part of the curriculum; for instance, language.

When influences on teaching practice are considered, it is also clear that the relative weights attached to the headteacher and to the school inspector/adviser differ. We argue that this is due to practical differences in their functions (see Chapter 3). English teachers feel that the school head is powerful, but not the school inspector/adviser. The situation is reversed in France, where the school inspector is felt to be the more powerful of the two, even though the inspectors' powers are felt to be somewhat limited.

But it is in the area of the influences and controls exercised by the users of the school (parents and pupils) that the differences between the two countries proved to be the most important. To summarize, the French conception is much more restricted and inward-looking. Both French and English teachers feel that it is essential to take into account the needs and characteristics of the local environment, and they both listen to what the families have to say, and profess their availability to them. But French teachers wish to remain in control, and be free to decide what to do with those possible influences, and are most reluctant to accord greater control to pupils and their families. This is not the case for the English teachers, who accept the validity of a wider range of influences which affect teaching practices.

These different conceptions of power and of the distribution of power were also manifest in the structural analysis of the questions relating to influences. For the French cohort these showed a clear distinction within teachers' perceptions between the influences relating to the school system and the influences relating to the families. For the English cohort, on the other hand, one dimension linked the influence of the school personnel with that of the parents, and another linked the influence of the personal experience of the teachers with the influence of the pupils. This implies a much more open and extended conception among the English teachers, one that integrates external influences, as opposed to the more restricted and inward-looking French conception.

This difference between the two cohorts has to be seen in the context of the general conception (extended or restricted) of the teacher's role which we discussed in Chapter 5. There we suggested that the English teachers placed much more emphasis on professional contact with other people (both from within and from outside the school). We can now say that in England not only do teachers see their job as giving them many opportunities for contact with others, they also feel that various other people have a much greater share of influence and control on the specific content of their teaching practice.

Chapter 10

A Network of Obligations

We saw in Chapter 7 that the notion of professional responsibility implies first of all the notion of accountability. This is what most English and French teachers in our study (approximately nine teachers in every ten) referred to when asked to explain what 'being professionally responsible' meant for them. Our task now is to look at this in more detail, and to see exactly to whom teachers felt they are accountable. We have for this purpose two kinds of data: the replies to the open-ended question mentioned above (Q. 18), and the replies to two types of closed questions – Questions 23.1 to 23.8 – which asked respondents to make use of a five-point scale in describing the accountability they felt to various persons and bodies: themselves and their own conscience; the headteacher; the parents; the school; the inspector; their own colleagues; their pupils and society in general. As before, in reviewing the responses made, we shall emphasize the comparisons between the two countries and the various locations of the schools.

GENERAL FINDINGS

Figure 10.1 shows responses concerning eight of the most frequently mentioned persons and bodies in the replies made concerning the focus for responsibility. The first interesting finding is that for both countries the vast majority of the teachers (over 90 per cent) said that they are accountable to their pupils. The second finding of note is that this is just about the only category mentioned for the French teachers. A fair number of the English teachers, however, said that they are accountable to their colleagues (29.3 per cent), to the parents (25.4 per cent), and to a smaller extent to their employer (12.7 per cent), to the headteacher (11.5 per cent), to their school (9.4 per cent), and to society in general (6.8 per cent). Here again, in the context of accountability, we have an overall difference which follows from the two different conceptions of the teacher's job (broad and restricted) mentioned many times before.

Another interesting finding is that, when talking of the same person or body, the teachers from both countries did this in a rather different fashion. For instance, the English teachers who talked of accountability to the parents of their pupils did this without any reservations, implying that this seemed to them entirely obvious and unavoidable. This feeling comes across in replies such as 'I feel responsible to parents

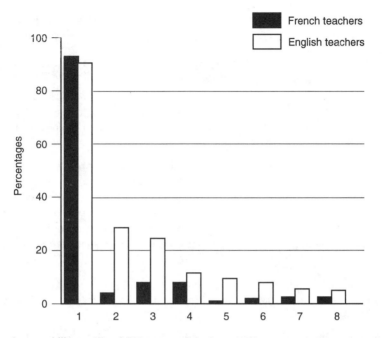

Figure 10.1 Accountability to whom? Percentage of teachers mentioning each of the following categories (open-ended question): 1, accountable to pupils; 2, accountable to colleagues; 3, accountable to parents; 4, accountable to employers; 5, accountable to headteacher; 6, accountable to the school; 7, accountable to myself; 8, accountable to society

for the education and instruction of their children', or 'My fourth responsibility is towards the parents . . . I understand their needs and try to cater for those needs to the best of my ability.' When the French teachers mentioned their accountability to parents, it was often with the underlying desire to justify themselves, or make the parents aware of their difficulties: 'I must make the parents aware of the realities of the teacher's job'; the idea of giving an account of something is there (the nature of the job, its difficulties), but there is nothing on accountability to parents for any educational objectives that the latter might be concerned about.

Another French teacher, talking about this job, even emphasized the neeed to dis-regard what parents might have to say:

> I have to do my job without taking into account the criticisms of parents relating to the teaching of spelling, of morals, of history. One simply cannot teach the same things as twenty or thirty years ago

Such a position is lucidly thought out, and even appears to exclude any possible compromise.

It does happen of course that some French teachers accept a greater measure of accountability to parents, but where this occurs it is rarely without any reservations, as is demonstrated by the reply of another French teacher: 'I feel responsible towards the parents who entrust me with the education of their children'; this particular reply seems to imply that there are two categories of parents: those who 'have complete trust in me', as they should, and the others who 'do not trust me' and to whom therefore the teacher is not accountable.

There are also differences where colleagues are concerned. Most of the replies of the

English teachers convey the idea of team spirit and collective responsibility in the way the job is conceived and done. One English teacher says, for instance:

> I am responsible to all of the teachers in the school, so that I do not do anything which might hinder my working relationship with my colleagues and with the children.

Or again, a headteacher says:

> I have a responsibility towards my colleagues to be *au fait* with new ideas and to ensure that they discuss them.

Another English teacher expresses very much the same idea when he says: 'I must behave in a professional fashion towards my colleagues.'

Such replies hardly ever occur for the French cohort. When accountability to colleagues is mentioned, in most cases it concerns the colleagues who teach the next class up, the overriding idea being to prepare adequately the pupils who will be in that class the following year. The following reply of a French teacher expresses this quite clearly:

> I am responsible to my colleagues, and must always therefore discharge my duties con-scientiously. I must not cause unnecessary work for the colleagues who will teach my pupils next year.

The replies to the closed questions (Table 10.1) confirm the above finding. Whilst the teachers from both cohorts recognize that they are accountable to their pupils, there are important differences in their feeling of accountability in other areas.

It is worth noting, however, that although very few teachers mentioned this of their own accord, both groups felt a strong degree of responsibility towards themselves and their own conscience when the precise question was actually put to them. The mean scores for the French cohort (4.8) and for the English cohort (4.9) are of the same order of magnitude as those relating to accountability to pupils (4.6 and 4.8 respectively).

The difference between the replies to the open-ended question and the closed question is not surprising. It seems reasonable to assume that, given the two areas of account-ability (to oneself and to the pupils), it is the feeling of responsibility towards the pupils which seems the most important, so that if the teachers rarely mention account-ability to their own conscience, it may be because they feel that such accountability goes without saying. Perhaps being responsible to one's pupils implies the idea of being responsible to one's own conscience to such an extent that it need not be mentioned. Certainly the fact that teachers tend to mention only their accountability to their pupils seems likely to be a reflection of their awareness of the overwhelming importance of attainment in school for the future of their pupils, although they also make it clear in other responses that they are very much aware of the fact that those results depend on the way they teach. Thus it might be argued that, as we shall see later, accountability to pupils and accountability to oneself are but two sides of the same coin. A feeling of responsibility towards one's pupils implies both an awareness of the importance of school results for the child, and an awareness of the teacher's role in this.

Turning to look in more detail at accountability to other persons and bodies, both within and outside the school, it is clear that the vast majority of French teachers (82 per cent) and of English teachers (89.5 per cent) said that it is their duty to explain to the parents the methods they use with their pupils (statement 25.4), and that many of them (although this is more so for the English teachers: 88.3 per cent compared with 70.8 per cent) felt that this is also the case for those in authority over them (statement

Table 10.1 *Accountability to whom? (fixed-response question). Mean scores (M) and standard deviations (SD)*

Accountable to:	French teachers		English teachers	
	M	SD	M	SD
Myself, my conscience	4.8	0.48	4.9	0.33
My pupils	4.6	0.68	4.8	0.53
The parents of my pupils	3.8	0.87	4.3	0.74
My school	3.7	1.54	4.2	0.71
Society in general	3.4	1.13	4.0	0.85
My colleagues	3.3	1.06	4.0	0.73
My inspector	3.0	1.12	3.0	0.95
My headteacher	2.7	1.21	4.2	0.61

25.17). The need to *inform* people other than those directly involved in the school is therefore widely accepted in both countries.

But accepting the need to explain teaching methods to someone not directly involved is one thing; feeling fully accountable to those 'outsiders' for the objectives to be reached is quite another. If we now go back to the closed questions (Table 10.1) concerning the importance of the feeling of accountability, we can see that there are differences between the two countries which follow the pattern of national differences already identified which relate to influence and control. As was the case with replies to the open-ended question, French teachers again appeared to feel less accountable than their English counterparts to their colleagues (mean score = 3.3 compared with 4.0), to their school (mean score = 3.7 compared with 4.2), and above all to their head (mean score = 2.7 compared with 4.2). Following the previous pattern, the least important person for the French teachers was the school's headteacher, and the inspector for the English teachers. Similarly, the French teachers felt less accountable than their English counterparts to the parents (mean score = 3.8 compared with 4.3) and to society (mean score = 3.4 compared with 4.0).

Perhaps the most significant finding here is the much greater emphasis placed by French teachers on their own conscience as a key regulator of professional responsibility. 'If I have done my best according to my own understanding of my role,' they appear to be saying, 'then it can't be my fault if the children fail'. Thus French teachers' greater degree of professional independence is manifest, as more of them (statement 25.6) felt that 'at the end of the day, teachers are only responsible to their own conscience' (59.8 per cent compared with 43.8 per cent), and also as less of them (statement 25.11) felt that 'a child's progress is not ultimately the responsibility of the teacher' (26 per cent compared with 43.8 per cent).

INFLUENCE OF THE LOCATION OF THE SCHOOLS

The general differences we have described between the two cohorts are valid regardless of the particular zones in which they teach. However, inner-city teachers in both countries were only half as likely as teachers in other areas to say that they are accountable to their employer and to the parents of their pupils. In France, there were still relatively fewer inner-city teachers, compared to their counterparts in other zones, who said they are accountable to persons or bodies not directly involved in the teaching, i.e. their school, society, the inspector and the school head. This point will be discussed further in the section that follows.

Underlying factors

The two factors: internal and external responsibilities

In discussing the picture that emerges from the factor analyses conducted on the closed questions it is important to bear in mind again the point that was made in Chapter 3, namely that these factors concern the relationship that exists *between* the responses made for the various statements rather than to the responses themselves.

The principal-components analysis of questions 23.1 to 23.8 on accountability produces interesting results. The first two components account for more than half of the total variance (51.3 per cent for the French cohort and 52.3 per cent for the English cohort). The first component includes all the people directly involved in the classroom, the only variables with a loading over 0.50 being for both countries and in the same order for both countries: accountability to the pupils (0.62 for the French cohort, 0.66 for the English cohort); and accountability to one's own conscience (0.56 for the French cohort, 0.50 for the English cohort). We shall describe this dimension, which is identical for both cohorts, as 'internal' accountability. Its existence confirms what was said earlier about the links between the feeling of accountability to the pupils and to oneself.

The second component covers accountability to persons and bodies not directly involved in the classroom. This we shall refer to as 'external' accountability. The highest loadings involve, for both countries, the six 'external' persons or bodies, and the lowest levels the two 'internal' persons or bodies, but with one interesting difference. In France, the three items with the highest loading are accountability to colleagues (0.72), to the school (0.72) and to the inspector (0.71). Then follow accountability to society (0.63) and to the school head (0.61). The last item is accountability to parents (0.51). In England, accountability to the inspector has the lowest loading (0.58) of the six items to do with the 'external' persons or bodies that teachers feel accountable to. On the other hand, accountability to parents is one of the three items with the highest loading (0.70), together with accountability to the school (0.76) and to colleagues (0.68). The two remaining items have loadings with values very similar to their values for the French dimension (0.65 for the school head, and 0.60 for society). In other words, 'external accountability' places more emphasis on parents and less emphasis on the inspector for the English cohort than it does for the French cohort, although it must be remembered that these are relative rather than absolute values, so that the actual responsibility felt in each case may be very different. This observation concerning accountability is very much in line with what was noted in relation to influences and control.

The results of the above analysis enable us to summarize the information provided by the eight variables, with just two types of scores, the first for internal or 'proximal' accountability, the second for external or 'distal' accountability. These scores were made up of the items with a loading over 0.50 (two for the former, six for the latter). These scores were then converted using a scale of 10, in order to facilitate comparisons. Table 10.2 gives the means and the standard deviations per zone for each country.

A quick glance at Table 10.2 shows that the feeling of internal responsibility is stronger than the feeling of external responsibility. This is in fact a condensed representation of the above findings for the individual items. The difference, however, is much more obvious for the French cohort. This is not due to differences concerning internal accountability, which is felt to a similarly high degree for both cohorts, but to differences concerning external accountability, which is felt to a much higher degree by the English cohort. The differences are considerable given the small range of dispersion.

Table 10.2 *'Internal' and 'external' responsibility: mean scores (M) and standard deviations (SD) for each factor*

Factors	Population			Zone 1: rural	Zone 2: working-class	Zone 3: inner city	Zone 4: middle-class	Total
				\multicolumn{5}{c}{Socio-economic zone of school}				
Internal responsibility	French	{	M	9.45	9.41	9.33	9.46	9.41
		{	SD	0.90	0.67	1.03	0.86	0.90
		{	No.	89	91	90	90	360
	English	{	M	9.58	9.67	9.71	9.69	9.67
		{	SD	0.74	0.65	0.56	0.63	0.65
		{	No.	85	86	88	87	346
External responsibility	French	{	M	6.48	6.72	6.21	6.93	6.60
		{	SD	1.21	1.23	1.48	1.44	1.37
		{	No.	89	91	90	90	360
	English	{	M	7.93	7.80	7.83	7.74	7.83
		{	SD	1.00	1.04	1.00	1.11	1.04
		{	No.	85	86	88	87	346

Whether we consider internal or external accountability, the spread of scores is also bigger for the French cohort, whatever the zone. In other words, there is less variation between teachers in the English cohort.

The influence of sex, age and the location of the schools

Compared to the influence of the country of origin, the influence of the other variables (age, sex and location of the schools) is small. The only factor which has a systematic and noticeable effect is external accountability (Table 10.3). Both in France and in England (although in a less obvious fashion for the latter), the feeling of external accountability increases with age, and is slightly greater among women teachers. In the French inner city there is a reduced concern for external accountability. This difference with the other zones may be partly due to the relative youth of the teachers in that zone, and to the fact that more of those teachers are male. Equally it may reflect the demands of the job itself and the perceived legitimacy or otherwise on the part of teachers working in such areas of common national regulations and expectations. Teaching according to one's *own* professional judgement of what the children need may indeed be an uncharacteristic but necessary response on the part of French teachers facing a far from typical professional challenge.

OVERVIEW

The data analysed above demonstrate the existence of both similarities and differences between the two school systems, the differences noted being very much in line with the observations made in the previous chapter concerning influences, constraints, and margins of freedom. The points are as follows.

Table 10.3   *External responsibility. Influence of (a) gender and (b) age: mean scores (M) and standard deviations (SD)*

(a) Influence of gender

	French teachers		English teachers	
	Males	Females	Males	Females
M	6.23	6.73	7.77	7.87
SD	1.53	1.27	1.07	1.03

(b) Influence of age

	French teachers			English teachers		
	<30 years	30–45 years	>45 years	<30 years	30–45 years	>45 years
M	5.93	6.47	6.93	7.37	7.87	7.93
SD	1.37	1.30	1.93	1.13	1.00	1.03

In both countries the feeling of accountability revolves around two main areas. The first is internal accountability which is centred around the classroom and the responsibility felt by the teacher towards the pupils and towards her own conscience. The second is external accountability felt by the teacher towards the other persons involved in the running of the school, the school itself, parents and society. Both English and French teachers feel a stronger sense of internal accountability, which they say is much more important. The nature of the moral contract which exists appears therefore to be essentially a contract between child and teacher. The dominant position of internal accountability appears to reflect both a deep awareness of the importance of school for children, and of the essential role of the teacher in ensuring that school is a successful experience for all children.

In relation to external responsibility, although French teachers do accept that they are accountable to persons or bodies other than themselves and their pupils, they still seem to have a rather more restrictive view: internal accountability is felt to be much more important than external accountability, whilst English teachers attach greater importance to both. For the English teachers much greater openness to, and awareness of, the other persons involved in the educational process (whether or not they are attached to the school), which we have already noted in discussing sources of influence and control, is therefore also present in the area of accountability. The English teachers exhibit a conception of their work which is much less inward-looking and 'centred on the self' than the French and have a more open attitude. We many speculate that these differences are in turn a reflection of the effects of the degree of central control within the system as this has influenced both the practice and the underpinning professional assumptions of teachers over the years. Furthermore, as we noted in relation to the discussion of influences and controls on teachers, the general socio-institutional factors outweigh other factors such as the teacher's age and sex. Although small, the influence of the teacher's age and sex was interesting since our data show that the feeling of external accountability increases slightly with age, and is slightly stronger among women teachers. A possible explanation is that increased maturity, and particularly the experience of family life, means that older teachers are more aware of the consequences and implications of their job for others. We also saw that inner-city teachers in both countries often feel less accountable to parents and to their employers than their colleagues from the other zones. This may be an effect of the relative lack of pressure from parents perceived by many inner-city teachers.

The factor analysis also confirmed that it is the French inner-city teachers who feel the least externally accountable, a fact which cannot be explained entirely by differences in age and sex. As we suggest, the explanation perhaps rests in the relative isolation of many French teachers faced with often difficult working conditions in the less privileged areas. If teachers are working with the belief that they are above all dependent on their own efforts with insufficient support from the school and the educational hierarchy, this could well lead to a decrease in the sense of responsibility felt towards outsiders.

Chapter 11

Conclusion

OVERVIEW

In the data presented in preceding chapters of this book we have discovered two very different professional profiles of primary school teaching. Our studies of teachers in France have shown them to have specific and relatively short-term goals for the children in their care, and to be teachers who tend to be formal in their pedagogy and isolated from outside influence in their daily contact with children. By contrast, teachers in England emerge as an occupational group with a much less clearly defined role. The goals they set for themselves are wide, even amorphous; they have, until recently, had no clear curriculum map to follow and to protect them from the conflicting demands of different social groups. They are enthusiastic and committed, often putting in a great deal more time than officially required to run extracurricular activities, to prepare challenging activities for children or to organize classroom displays of children's work. Thrown to a considerable extent on their own initiative in deciding what and how to teach, English teachers are typically supported by close working and social relations with colleagues and the leadership of the headteacher.

In addition to these very significant differences, however, our research has revealed a common core of professionalism which is shared by both groups and which is centred on an intense commitment to children as the primary focus of the teacher's concern. Both French and English teachers appear to be strongly motivated by a sense of moral responsibility which makes them feel obligated to do the best they can, as they see it, for their pupils (Nias, 1989). In consequence, both groups of teachers are likely to resist any attempt by less significant 'others' - notably in the form of changes in government policy - which they see as potentially inimical to the fulfilment of this primary goal.

Although it is this latter finding which has perhaps the most practical significance for the future - as we shall discuss later in this chapter - it is important to take the detailed comparisons we have reported in this book as a whole to understand fully the rich and novel insights they provide about the nature of teaching and how it may be studied. Thus in what follows we briefly summarize the main findings of our research and consider some of the theoretical and practical implications which arise from them.

SUMMARY OF MAIN FINDINGS

Part of our enquiry was designed to elicit descriptive, factual information about the teachers themselves which was potentially relevant to their professional life. In this respect we asked about such things as age, sex, professional experience and home circumstances.

Not surprisingly we found that primary teaching in both countries was dominated by women. Within this broad generalization, however, there was a very clear tendency in France for older, usually female teachers to gravitate towards the affluent suburban schools, leaving the schools in difficult social areas to the young and inexperienced teachers, many more of whom were men. In Chapter 5 we explained this finding by referring to the French promotion structure, which is based largely on age and experience, coupled with the inflexibility of teaching goals and techniques which makes the task of teaching one which is substantially 'easier' in favoured social areas. No such clear pattern of a 'flight to the suburbs' existed in the English study.

The variability of teaching practice which appears to be more characteristic of the English is reflected too in their more diverse and typically more lengthy training. It is also reflected in the range of different 'special responsibility' posts available in school compared with the largely undifferentiated role of the former *instituteur*, now *professeur d'école*, in France. Nevertheless, French and English teachers work in broadly similar physical environments although the French teacher typically has a much smaller class – around 22 as against the English 30. Their classes are also more homogeneous in terms of achievement level since almost a third of French pupils have to repeat one or more school years at some point because they have not reached the necessary standard to move up.

The English teacher is thus faced with the task of meeting a wide variety of learning needs in a large class which may also include a wide span of ages and achievement levels. By contrast the French teacher may have to deal with the low self-esteem of pupils who are repeated failures – a contrast which has particular pertinence in difficult social areas, where the English teachers' opportunity to match their teaching to what they perceive their pupils' needs to be can make the problem of teaching in these areas less difficult than in France, where the existence of standardized curriculum objectives has led to very high levels of year repetition.

In Chapters 5 and 6 we also discussed the social and professional relations and working environment characteristic of teaching in the two countries. We found the French teacher working largely independently of colleagues and of the headteacher except in the more challenging circumstances of difficult social areas. The English teacher, by contrast, accepted it as normal to collaborate with colleagues and looked to both colleagues and headteacher for professional support and to the latter for leadership. This greater permeability, or openness to other influences, of English professional practice was also reflected in the frequent presence of parents in the classroom and in the readiness to enlist their help for a variety of activities. The French teacher's not infrequent exchanges with parents tended to be more formal and concerned with a child's academic progress. Again marked variations were noted in this respect from one socio-economic zone to another, French teachers in disadvantaged areas finding it particularly difficult to make contact with parents. As regards contact with other professionals, this was minimal in both countries and confined very much to educational problems and strategies. Whatever teachers' worries might be about pupils' progress, these rarely seemed to be reflected in non-educational discussions and solutions.

These necessarily highly selective data on the objective conditions of teachers' working lives nevertheless provide a clear picture of the differences which are produced at the level of the individual teachers and their ideology and practice by the degree of centralization of the education system. In sum they suggest strongly that centralization is likely to disadvantage less favoured socio-economic groups since teachers working to common, public goals cannot hope to achieve the same levels of 'success' in such areas and yet are not allowed to adapt their goals better to meet these pupils' needs. The result, as the French experience suggests, is likely to be frustration and a sense of failure among both pupils and teachers. Conversely, it may be that the English teacher's readiness to adapt teaching goals to meet the needs of inner-city children carries with it the inherent risk of lower expectations for these children, leading ultimately to a lower level of achievement than that of which they are capable.

Part III of our report took us into the minds of the teachers to explore their goals, their obligations and their perceived constraints. Of the many interesting comparisons in this section none is more significant than the finding that both French and English teachers are first and foremost committed to their pupils. For the French, this commitment takes the form of concern, in the first instance, about academic progress and successful completion of the year by each pupil, although the longer-term inculcation of skills needed for adult life also figures significantly. For the English, the commitment is much broader, embracing children's social and emotional development as well as their academic progress, and including also a concern to promote enjoyment of the learning process on a day-to-day basis.

In Chapter 7 we identified three broad factors which characterize teachers' overall feelings about their job: idealism, realism and 'social openness'. We found that both sets of teachers have no illusions about the difficulties of teaching – the lack of value placed upon it by society, the lack of resources, the very nature of the 'job' itself – and yet they retain their fundamental commitment to children and to the 'vocational' aspect of teaching. Where the populations differ, as might be anticipated, is with respect to their openness to outside influences.

With regard to other sources of influence of which teachers are aware, both groups appear to rate personal experience, their pupils and their own study as important, with professional training rated as relatively unimportant. Within this broad consensus, the English teachers see the school – in the shape of the head, colleagues and participation in extracurricular activities and their own ideology – as important influences, whereas for French teachers it is the extra-institutional influences of the inspector and the union which are, predictably, more significant.

As well as the variety of subtle influences that affect teachers, there are the more direct sources of constraint and control which also affect teachers' practice. English teachers, as might be expected, appeared at the time of the study to enjoy much greater freedom in this respect even in the central matter of curriculum content in the core subjects of mathematics and language. Such freedom may be, in part at least, why English teachers appear to take a much more democratic view of teaching than their French counterparts, being prepared to be open to a wide range of outside contacts and influences which they allow to impinge on their professional practice.

There are no systematic zone differences which modify these national typifications or alter the pride of place given by both groups of teachers to the internal responsibility that centres on self and pupils, rather than the external focus of school, parents, system and society. Surprisingly, however, it is the more egocentric French teacher, sure of her goals and not accustomed to looking for institutional support, who is less likely to feel obligated to other members of the education system in a sense of formal accountability. Her accountability to her pupils and to her own sense of professionalism is expressed in fulfilling the system's expectations. There is no need for another language, another channel of communication.

THEORETICAL PERSPECTIVES

A great deal of intellectual effort has been expended in recent years in trying to theorize about the nature and interrelationship of the various forms of influence and control which impinge on teachers – forms of the kind we have explored empirically in our research. Kogan (1984) distinguishes between *bureaucratic accountability*, such as that of a managerial hierarchy; *professional control*, which is self-evaluating and autonomous; and *consumerist control*, which leaves teachers accountable directly to the public, especially parents. This analysis offers a starting point. It does not, however, emphasize the subjective dimension of professionalism, that sense of personal responsibility which has emerged as central in our study and which Becher *et al.* (1981) claim is the least amenable to external pressures for change. ·

> Teachers perceive their accountability in ways which are related to the differences in how they identify their roles, organise their classes and assess their pupils. Implicit models of accountability are ingrained into the way they think and behave – they may even be part of their personalities. This natural system of personal accountability is unlikely to be easily altered by formal changes in accountability procedures.

It is this relationship between self-imposed as distinct from various forms of externally imposed constraints, the various threads of responsibility and accountability, influence and control to which teachers are subject, which formed the focus for our study. In this respect our findings reinforce the conceptualizations arising from previous British studies (e.g. Elliott *et al.*, 1981; Munn *et al.*, 1982 – a Scottish study), that for some teachers accountability was essentially hierarchical, a 'control' model that meant 'having one's actions determined by another's pre-set expectations or fitting in with the role expectations determined by others'. But for others it was a much more self-imposed 'dialogue' that meant 'accepting responsibility for one's own decisions and actions whilst encouraging others to exert a rational influence through criticism and discussion'.

Given that most of the existing literature on professional responsibility is English or American, it is not surprising that most favour 'professional' rather than bureaucratic modes of control, arguing that the former is more likely to lead to realization in action than hierarchical directives, which can only be enforced with difficulty. This is not to say, however, that one approach is more benign than another or is likely to favour a particular set of social values.

> the question of what values lurk behind different schemes has been confused by the ascription of particular motives to particular organisational forms. . . . It does not follow that public control will necessarily be tied up with inequality, oppressive hierarchies, or industrially oriented educational systems. . . . In principle, systems are ethically neutral: the group who control them can use them, and their associated rhetoric, to advance any value mix they choose . . .
>
> (Kogan, 1984)

This point is well brought out by a comparison between England and France. Where English educational traditional emphasizes the sanctity of the individual and his rights, French educational tradition emphasizes the contrasting value of central control as the guarantee of equality and national unity. As Kogan points out, a public control system does ultimately rest on a political mandate. In contrast, under the 'professional accountability' mode so staunchly championed by British educationists, 'teachers become in effect an elite protected from accountability to the elected political leadership' (Kogan, 1984).

The defensibility of such a stance was explicitly brought into question by Kenneth Baker when he was Secretary of State for Education:

> Is it really acceptable that in the vital matter of education hardly anyone can be sure about where responsibilities really lie?. . . . Above all, is it acceptable that the customers of the system, who find the bulk of the money, should be quite unable to judge these claims against each other because they too are not sure what our schools set out to achieve? We cannot continue with a system under which teachers decide what pupils should learn without reference to clear, nationally agreed objectives and without having to expose and, if necessary, justify their decisions to parents, employers and the public.

At the heart of this debate are fundamental issues about the optimum means of delivering national educational provision. A decade or more of research into various aspects of accountability has provided powerful, albeit anglocentric, theoretical frameworks with which to address the key questions of quality control and target setting.

The notion of 'accountability', as we now understand it, allows a distinction to be drawn between the source, strength and currency of different influences upon teachers' practice. The concept of responsibility, however, starts from a more psychological concern with the mediated reality of that objective situation in the teacher's own consciousness. That is to say, the starting point is reality as conceived by the teacher and as reflected in the action she constructs in accordance with this conception of responsibility. Responsibility then may be seen as the internalized, articulated product of diverse strands of accountability, which, in turn, inform the beliefs which allow teachers to function in their particular educational setting.

Our findings suggest that it is this latter source of professional direction which is critical in determining what teachers do and which will therefore be of critical importance in predicting the success or otherwise of efforts to implement changes in the system. Whilst in a very real sense, as we have shown, teachers are the product of the education system in which they work, the system is also, in consequence, continually being reproduced by them. This is because teachers' educational ideology, their view of what they are trying to achieve and how they may best achieve it is likely to be deeply influenced by their own educational experience as pupils and the 'role models' they have encountered at that stage. As we have shown, it is these deeply rooted assumptions about teaching which are a major source of inertia in the education system.

Many researchers writing in the British and American traditions have seen the recent increasing centralization of education in both countries as a form of de-professionalization' and 'de-skilling' since it limits the teacher's margin of manoeuvre (Lawn and Ozga, 1981; Apple, 1986). This tradition of autonomy and moral responsibility is associated with high professional status. Yet it is arguable that the very professional autonomy so cherished by teachers in decentralized systems has been associated with a tendency to embrace an 'extended' notion of professionalism (Hoyle, 1973) or 'professionality' in which the teacher is committed to

> seeing his work in the wider context of community and society, ensuring that his work is informed by theory, research, and current exemplars of good practice; being willing to collaborate with other teachers in teaching, curriculum development, and the formation of school policy, and having a commitment to keeping himself professionally informed.

All too often this can result in conflict between the standards teachers set themselves and what they can realistically achieve (MacPherson, 1972). By contrast, traditionally more authoritarian systems, where the long experience of detailed curriculum prescription, pedagogic guidelines and regular inspection has served to contain professional definitions of responsibility within much narrower limits, have arguably made these responsibilities more achievable. Far from resulting in reduced professional satisfaction, enforced focusing can help to increase it. This is because, as our evidence suggests, in England and France at least, teachers' self-imposed moral responsibility is likely to centre on a 'high level of classroom competence, teaching skill and good relationships with pupils' – what Hoyle terms 'restricted' professionalism in which teachers derive most of their sense of role fulfilment from intrinsic work factors. Nias (1986) identifies similar dimensions in a study in which teachers stressed the importance of 'being whole', 'being themselves', being natural and establishing deeply felt relationships with children. However, this will be more likely to be the case *if teachers themselves* accept the desirability of this kind of control and the narrow version of professional responsibility with which it is likely to be associated. Furthermore, although it may lead to higher job satisfaction, the tendency for teachers to retreat into this narrow version of professionalism when operating within tight bureaucratic structures which inhibit innovation may also have the associated disadvantage of inhibiting the broader and more flexible definition of goals which our data suggest may be in the best interests of disadvantaged children. The truth of this is well demonstrated by the current difficulties in French education in providing for such pupils, which was referred to above.

The research we have reviewed here suggests clearly the tension between 'restricted' and 'extended' notions of professionalism and the importance of teachers' own ideology in determining which they find the most fulfilling.

Thus, we would argue that particular modes of accountability and control cannot be directly equated with more or less professionalism; that although 'restricted' professionality focuses more sharply on the core responsibilities of classroom interaction and may therefore make job satisfaction easier to achieve in principle, the major determinant of job satisfaction is how closely the working conditions a teacher experiences allow her to realize her responsibilities in a way that accords with her own educational ideology. Thus for French primary teachers, their preferred 'restricted' view of professional responsibility is currently under threat from changing pupil, and hence social needs and policy initiatives on the part of government aimed at changing teachers' practice better to meet these needs. For English primary teachers, the autonomy over curriculum and teaching methods which has been a central feature of their professional responsibility is under the contrasting threat of government initiatives which also require them to narrow their focus on the 'whole child' to more strictly academic objectives.

This sense of professionalism is far removed from that more formal notion of profession identified earlier in which the key criteria are restrictive entry and esoteric knowledge. In this latter sense, Hoskin (1977) rightly argues that the Impérial Université revived by Napoleon in nineteenth-century France made school teaching the archetypal profession in terms of its fulfilment of the criteria of monopoly, service and expertise, but this says little about how those same teachers actually conceived of their 'professional' responsibility. By the same token, the continuing commitment of the vast majority of French teachers to the desirability of central control of curriculum and pedagogy, evaluation and employment does not make them less 'professional' than their more decentralist colleagues. It serves rather to stress the dangers of ethnocentricity in this respect and the consequent importance of establishing prima facie what may be very different dimensions of professional responsibility. These constitute the active realization of the diverse external and ideological influences and constraints of any one educational system. It follows from this, too, that teachers themselves will be likely to judge their success in different ways according to these broad conceptions of their professional responsibility.

When a very wide range of objectives makes it difficult, or even impossible, to gauge how successful a teacher has been in realizing these objectives, it is correspondingly more likely that the teacher will impose less moral responsibility on herself for the long-term outcomes. In effect it is the activities, the *process* of teaching and learning itself, that are the primary focus for such a teacher's professional responsibility rather than the *products* of the relatively unreflective, unproblematic teaching which is the focus for a narrower definition of professional responsibility.

Three points emerge from this discussion. First it is clear that there are no absolute value judgements to be made about the desirable components of professional responsibility. Instead it is important to establish the implications of any one approach and how these may be affected by any particular national context. Secondly, it is important to map that large area of professional common ground that all teachers share, regardless of tradition, since it is inherent in the nature of teaching itself.

A third and final point may be extrapolated from these two. This concerns potential intra-national variations which are a response to significant variations in the cultural context of teaching despite the common impulses of the over-arching national system.

Any attempt to improve teaching must necessarily involve an attempt to elucidate systematically these three dimensions of professional ideology. It must go beyond an objective mapping of the network of controls and influence to which any particular teacher would appear to be subject and start instead from the self-imposed goals and standards which act as a day-to-day professional conscience in influencing the way teachers carry out their role. Although essentially self-imposed, these goals and standards are also likely to include those formal, contractual requirements imposed on the teacher by external agencies. Whilst explicitly educational instructions might be the most obvious element in this, other, less obvious dimensions need to be taken into account, such as 'civic' responsibility concerned with rules regarding pupil supervision and safety and even 'judicial' responsibility concerned with sanctions against physical, mental, sexual or other forms of abuse against pupils. In addition there may be specific dimensions of bureaucratic responsibility associated with the management of a particular institution.

The nature of these perceived contractual responsibilities, combined with the many less formal obligations the teacher feels obliged to fulfil in order to meet her own definition of what is expected of her by interested parties such as colleagues, pupils and parents, will determine the dimensions of behaviour which she and others regard as 'professional'. In England the degree of autonomy which teachers at the time of this study were conscious of possessing in both setting and attempting to realize their objectives is taken to be a defining characteristic of professionalism. In France this 'margin of manoeuvre' is relatively insignificant in comparison with teachers' stress on their obligation to pupils in fulfilling the task that has been entrusted to them.

As Sockett *et al.* (1984) argue in trying to define a professional model of teacher accountability, definitions of professionalism can emphasize *results* as the focus of responsibility – as in France – either short-term or long-term, or they can emphasize the equally important dimension of the *quality of experiences* and conditions which that teacher provides. Our findings suggest that it is this latter aspect that is the primary focus for English teachers' professionalism.

Such contrasts illustrate the fatuity of trying to define, once and for all, the 'good teacher' in anything but the narrowest, decontextualized, psychological sense (Hammersley, 1980). As Hargreaves (1986) puts it:

> Teaching is certainly a matter of competence. But it is competence of a particular kind. It is the competence to recognise and enact the rules, procedures and forms of understanding of a particular cultural environment. What is involved is not technical competence to operate in a pre-given, professionally correct and educationally worthwhile way, but cultural competence to 'read' and 'pass' in a system with its own specific history; a system once devised and developed to meet a very particular set of social purposes.

IMPLICATIONS FOR PRACTICE

The existence of specific national traditions of professionalism reinforces the supreme importance of understanding how teachers see their professional responsibility, before any attempt can be made to *change* the nature of their practice. Crude attempts, such as we are currently witnessing in England, to make teachers more contractually accountable and, by so doing, to steer more directly their practice, can thus be shown to be largely doomed to failure unless teachers' *own* definitions of their professional responsibility also change. The data presented here suggest that such a change might not be wholly undesirable from the English teachers' point of view, in making them less at the mercy of outside influences and in limiting their goals in a way that allows for a greater sense of achievement.

Indeed it is debatable who currently has the greatest crisis in morale: the French *professeur d'école* who, tied to a traditional curriculum which may have little relevance or appeal for many pupils, has neither the right nor the skill to change it, or the English primary teacher who sets herself the unachievable goal of an individualized pedagogy in a class of over 30 pupils and who has no clear idea of the limits of her responsibility.

For pupils, what is the impact of coping, as they do in France, with an impersonal, often harsh pedagogy and an often arid curriculum, as compared to a typically more liberal, but highly varying, set of teacher expectations as in England? Is it the case, as Bernstein (1977) has argued, that the very adaptability of a child-centred pedagogy, for all its apparent attractions, makes pupils far more vulnerable to the perpetuation of inequality?

These and other questions are prompted by the evidence of consistent national differences in the conceptions of professional responsibility held by teachers in the two countries studied. In some cases, this evidence reflects cultural assumptions which are so pervasive that they are never articulated. But although this unspoken collective consciousness is deeply significant it is important to set against it the intra-societal differences between socio-economic zones which have been referred to in this book. It is these comparisons which, in the study reported here, have provided for more specialized micro-international comparisons as well as providing the yardstick against which to assess the significance of national stereotypes compared to local, institutional and individual variations. Our evidence testifies to the overwhelming importance of system-specific ideology as a determinant of teachers' conceptions of their professional responsibility. Indeed it points to French teachers' *belief* in the need for a national curriculum as the basis for equality and unity in their society, rather than any external constraint, as the key to its impact.

Arguably, however, teachers have always been subject to greater control in England, susceptible as they are to pressure from consumers – notably parents – and a range of exhortations emanating from within the school, the local authority and at national level. The passionately held commitment of most primary teachers in England and Wales to professional autonomy in both curriculum and pedagogy, the freedom of the individual school to decide how to educate its children, and the child-centred ideology which supports a pedagogy that aspires to be individualist are all ideals held at the cost of a not inconsiderable personal sacrifice among English teachers. If they were to accept a narrower, more universal and common curriculum, they would probably find themselves with a greater sense of achievement, being less vulnerable to outside criticism, and possibly even having a higher status in society. However, it is the ideology or, to put it another way, the conception of their professional role which plays the most fundamental part in determining what teachers do. If policy changes ride roughshod over such ideologies, and fail to take them into account, the result is likely to be widespread resentment, a lowering of morale and, possibly, a reduced effectiveness. Findings from a more recent survey of teachers in England (Osborn and Broadfoot, 1992b) confirm this prediction.

A much more profitable strategy would be to set in motion a process of self-examination within the teaching profession itself in the light of the kind of data we have presented here. As part of this, teachers would be invited to address the assumptions underpinning the ideology of autonomy and the potential advantages for themselves of more clearly defined expectations of their role. It could even be that teachers would recognize that having a minimum structure – the framework of a national curriculum devised by teachers themselves – might provide both support and protection within which they could still work in relative professional freedom. Simply to impose a national curriculum and attainment targets on teachers is most unlikely to work in the same way that it does in France even if that were the desired goal. Rather, all the recognized disadvantages of the French system – its rigidity and inflexibility, its narrowness and limited relevance to much of modern life – would be likely to be added to the widespread resentment and disquiet felt by teachers who are constrained to adopt a professional role that is alien to them. The same strategy might be applied towards the opposite goal in France. Teachers might be invited to consider the potential benefits of more institutional freedom and a less rigid promotion structure.

It is significant that recent French educational policy has moved towards a decentralization of educational provision and, at least in primary schools, to a considerable strengthening of the power of the headteacher. These apparent moves to breaking down the traditional monopoly of central government reflect a recognition that central government direction in the form it is currently exercised has not been effective enough in ensuring a high-quality educational product. In the view of the French teacher unions, this change, in which heads will now be selected by the *recteur d'académie* – who is in turn the political nominee of central government – and not, as in the past, by offering themselves for appointment on the grounds of length of service, may well provide for more effective imposition of centrally determined policies than hitherto.

More generally, however, this kind of carefully controlled decentralization can be seen as a response to the urgent need to overcome some of the disadvantages associated with strong central control of education. Prominent in this respect is the difficulty of promoting curriculum development and new approaches to teaching in a system where conformity has long been the norm. This lesson is an important one which current British government policy seems to be bent on ignoring.

In England the 1988 Education Reform Act embodies many fallacies. It casts the curriculum in terms of 'what pupils should be able to know, do and understand'; it assumes that to study and to learn are the same thing; that all pupils should pursue the same 'attainment targets' and at the same pace; and that the existence of universal competition will motivate, rather than demoralize, the majority of children. French experience contradicts these assumptions. As the *redoublement* figures we cite in Chapter 4 indicate, many teachers are finding it increasingly difficult to promote successful learning among children whose backgrounds offer little support for what the education system is trying to do for them. Yet the notion of a common entitlement remains strongly supported by most French teachers. How much more difficult to implement is a national assessment system in England where teachers in primary schools at least believe their professional responsibilities ought to be exercised according to an ideology of individual pupil need and interest?

A study of the context of teaching such as we have presented here can play a vital role in distinguishing the elements that influence the subjectivity of professionalism within the context of a particular education system. It can also reveal how complex is the relationship between making decisions about pedagogy, curriculum and assessment and that of achieving pupil outcomes, and the dilemmas, even agonies, inherent in this process.

Any attempt to understand teachers' professional motivation must address the interaction between the influence of the teaching situation itself – the impact of a particular socio-psychological environment characterized by factors such as unequal authority relations, pupil coercion and group-oriented curricula – and those nationally specific influences involving traditions and ideology which are mediated by the day-to-day manipulations of policy-makers and administrators. The personal influences of teachers' careers, experience and training, personality and attitude add a further layer of variation. The broad systemic differences we have identified above necessarily obscure a good deal of this variation. They also do not address the potentially substantial disjuncture between intention and action so well documented in other studies such as those of Sharp and Green (1975) and Keddie (1971), although the data reported briefly in Chapter 6 confirm that classroom practice broadly reflects the major differences in approach to teaching among teachers in the two countries reported here. However, this national difference in teachers' perceptions renders problematic ethnocentrically inspired notions of professionalism in teaching and underlines the relativity of what constitutes 'good' teaching in a given context.

The familiar stereotypes of the two national education systems under study are borne out by the data reported here. The French one is still characterized by a formal curriculum and strong central direction; the English one retains a more integrated curriculum approach and institutional autonomy. Both systems, however, are responding to major changes in the social context of education at the present time. These changes are challenging policy-makers to address the contradictions present in both systems concerning how good teaching can be promoted without forfeiting control of educational outcomes.

In recent years, the British government has given a great deal of attention to measures aimed at improving the quality of teachers and teaching. The institution of teacher appraisal, the provision of incentive allowances, the identification of national priority areas for in-service education for teachers, local financial management of schools and the significant strengthening of consumer choice under the 1988 Education Reform Act reflect a policy climate committed to improving educational quality through giving schools the means and the obligation to respond to market forces whilst strengthening the overall control of the education system from the centre.

The lessons from France, however, suggest that whilst such moves may result in some reduction in the strains experienced by teachers who embrace an extended professionalism, problematic goals, a process orientation and a particularistic pedagogy, they are also likely to pose new problems. The assumption found in French education, that both the means and the ends of the educational process can and should be generalized, may relieve teachers of the burden of choice but in so doing it reduces both their ability and their willingness to respond to different local and pupil needs. It is the recognition of this limitation that lies behind current French moves to increase personal and institutional autonomy within the education system.

The depth of the current crisis within French education is reflected in the fact that some estimates suggest perhaps half of all school leavers are unable to read and write satisfactorily, despite the huge expenditure on education. For this reason education now has pride of place in government policy, the Education Minister now ranking above even the Finance and Foreign Ministers in the Cabinet (Geddes, 1982).

Our research has demonstrated that it is their deeply held convictions which enable primary teachers to resolve the diverse and heavy demands that their chosen profession makes upon them. The exhaustion, the lack of public recognition, the frustration of too many children and too few resources, and the elusive sense of achievement can nevertheless be borne where the teacher is able to feel she is doing a good job, where she can live up to her own professional image – where she can sustain her own confidence and self-esteem. As Nias (1989) suggests:

> The feelings associated with teaching seem always to be contradictory. Successful teachers learn to keep them in balance, but even they swing, sometimes by the minutes, between love and rage, elation and despair. To 'be' a teacher is to be relaxed and in control, yet tired and under stress, to feel whole while being pulled apart; to be in love with one's work, but daily to talk of leaving it. It is to learn to live with unresolved uncertainties, contradictions and dilemmas; to accept that the very nature of teaching is paradoxical.

Thus we must conclude from the evidence presented in this book that both countries are seeking to introduce some elements of the strengths of the other. As Broadfoot (1982a) suggested, both countries appear to be moving towards a combination of central prescription *and* product-based accountability. This is essentially a belt-and-braces approach which Neave (1988) associates with the new evaluative state in which accountability for centrally determined criteria for practice is devolved to semi-independent units of the education system. The programme of budgetary deconcentration which has been going on for some time in France is as much a reflection of this new approach to making control effective as is the introduction of local financial management in England and the publication of league tables.

Both attempts at reform ignore the international evidence that now exists that educational change cannot be brought about simply by manipulating institutional structures or issuing policy directives. Furthermore they fail to take into account the significant drop in morale that is likely to accompany any attempt to force teachers to change their practice. A study by Webb and Ashton (1987) in the United States argues that teacher efficacy is currently threatened by seven key factors: excessive role demands; poor remuneration and status; lack of recognition and professional isolation; uncertainty about success; a sense of powerlessness to control the work environment; alienation; and a rapid drop in teacher morale. A major cause of this situation, Webb and Ashton argue, is the attempt to 'individualize' reform – to blame individual teacher inadequacy for the shortcomings of the system. 'Teachers' instructional strategies are highly resistant to change' they suggest. 'Tackling this sensitive area of teacher autonomy, before addressing the more pressing problems of the conditions of teaching, will result in unmitigated disaster.' Achieving change in education, as Fullan (1991) has pointed out, involves changing what teachers think and what teachers do; it is as simple and as complex as that. In France, the industrial unrest in response to the 1989 Jospin reform package, which has not been quelled even by the promise of large salary increases, suggests that any attempt at change which fails to take into account the real influences on teachers' professional motivation and practice will be unsuccessful in all respects but one. It may well succeed in eroding the professional commitment inherent in working towards self-imposed goals which is the explicit core of the motivation of both cohorts of teachers in the study reported here. Only then, when it is too late, will the real key to effective educational change be apparent.

The government rhetoric produced so far in both countries takes little account of such contradictions. Nor has it even tried to establish in terms of academic and social outcomes whether the kind of system it seeks to emulate does in fact produce the desired results. In England the picture of the typical French classroom in which chalk and talk/didactic teaching predominates may appeal to many traditionalists. It should appeal also to many English teachers, for it is certainly less demanding to execute. The fact that it does not appear to appeal, at least to most primary teachers, needs to be explained. Why do English primary teachers continue to struggle with the impossible task they set themselves? Certainly not for any extrinsic reward or for public approbation or ease of execution. Perhaps it has something to do with their experience of working with children, and of responding to their individual needs; from witnessing children's pleasure in their own creativity, which was the core of professional motivation of the primary teachers in this study. In France, similarly, the widespread opposition and industrial action which greeted the Education Minister's decree appointing heads for primary schools also show clearly the folly of trying to promote changes at policy level without taking into account the deeply held convictions of teachers about how their professional role should be exercised.

This study has given clear confirmation of the truth of this statement. It follows then that if change in education is to be successfully implemented, much more attention than hitherto needs to be given to considering *ways of changing how teachers think*, which will in turn impact upon what they do. All too often, however, directives are concerned with changing what teachers *do* without taking any account of how teachers' thinking might need to change if such changes are to be seen as acceptable and thus become incorporated as part of teachers' own internal professional goals.

The need to forestall such developments emphasizes the value of cross-national comparisons of the kind reported here, which offer virtually the only guide to potential outcomes. There is clearly an urgent need, for example, to conduct a complementary study of pupil outcomes in the two systems. Such a study is needed in order to examine the significance of the major differences in teaching approaches that we have identified in this work and to challenge the assumptions about how to raise standards that appear to be informing current policy initiatives in both countries. International, bilingual research projects face particular problems of ensuring both comparability and validity in their methodology. Nevertheless it should be apparent from the data reported here how valuable such studies can be as a basis for policy-making and for opening up new theoretical perspectives.

Appendix 1

The Questionnaire

Bristol–Aix study: Conceptions of professional responsibility among French and English teachers

Please place a tick in the appropriate box. In cases where a question is clearly not relevant to you, please draw a line through it or write N.A. (not applicable).

A. GENERAL INFORMATION

1. What is the approximate number of pupils in your school? ☐

2. About what percentage of pupils belong to the following cultural groups?

   British: approximate percentage ☐

   Other: approximate percentage ☐

What is/are the main non-British groups?

_____

_____

3. Which of the following describes the area in which your school is situated?

   Rural area, e.g. market town, village ☐

   A suburban area with a high proportion of manual workers and/or clerical white collar workers ☐

   An inner city area with a high proportion of ethnic minorities and often poor housing conditions ☐

   An urban area which is mainly middle-class: good housing conditions; a high proportion of managerial/executive occupations, the liberal professions, and intellectuals ☐

   Other. Please describe ☐

_____

_____

4. What is the number of pupils in your class?

	Boys	Girls	Total
	☐	☐	☐

5. Which year group are you responsible for as a classroom teacher? Tick all which apply.

1st year junior ☐

2nd year junior ☐

3rd year junior ☐

4th year junior ☐

6. In your class, how many pupils are:

– younger than the normal age for this class ☐

– the normal age for this class ☐

– older than the normal age for this class by 1 year ☐

by 2 years ☐

ACADEMIC LEVEL

7. Estimate the number of pupils in your class who are, in relation to age norms:

Above average in ability ☐

Average in ability ☐

Below average in ability ☐

8. What is your position in the school?

Head ☐

Deputy head ☐

Post with special responsibility ☐

Classroom teacher only ☐

Other (please specify) ☐

_____

9. Do you work:

Full-time ☐

Part-time ☐

10. Are you:

Permanent? ☐

Temporary? ☐

B. PRACTICES, CONCEPTIONS, POINTS OF VIEW

11.   Do you organize or co-ordinate any extracurricular activities? e.g. school clubs, games, workshops, choir, school camp/school trips, etc.

Yes	No
☐	☐

If yes, please specify _____

_____

_____

_____

_____

12.   In the past year, how frequently have you had personal contact with each of the following in the course of your work as a teacher?

Contact	Degree of contact			
	1–3 times a month or more	Once or twice a term	Once or twice a year	Never
1. School governor				
2. Local inspector/adviser				
3. LEA administrator/ elected representative				
4. Educational psychologist				
5. Visiting remedial teacher				
6. Social worker				
7. School doctor				
8. Psychotherapist, speech therapist, or other				

13a.   How often do you work in close collaboration with a colleague or colleagues when teaching your class or another group of pupils?

Never	☐
Less than once a week	☐
Once a week	☐
More than once a week	☐
Daily or almost daily	☐

13b.   What form would this collaboration take?

_____

_____

14.   In the course of your professional work, what type of contact do you have with the parents of your pupils and how frequently?

In the course of my work, I have contact with parents:	How often					
	Never	Less than once a month	At least once a month	Once a week	Several times a week	Daily or almost daily
1. To help with classroom activities						
2. When meeting to discuss a child's progress						
3. To organize together social or recreational activities: concerts, fetes, etc.						
4. At PTA meetings						
5. By individual letter/telephone call						
6. To accompany children on school trips and visits						
7. When meeting by chance						
8. Other (specify)						

15, 16. Here is a list of methods and procedures which can be used in evaluating the results of your work with pupils. Question 15 asks about whether these methods exist in your class, and Question 16 asks how important you feel these methods of evaluation to be, whether or not they are used in your class.

Methods of Evaluation		15. Existence of these methods of evaluation				16. Importance for you of these methods of evaluation				
		Often used	Sometimes used	Seldom used	Never used	Very important	Important	Fairly important	Fairly unimportant	Not important at all
Your own procedures	1. Without tests									
	2. With personal tests									
	3. With standard-ized tests									
4. Evaluation by a visiting professional with tests										
5. Evaluation by the head or a colleague who is a subject specialist										
6. Group discussion with other teachers										
7. Evaluation by the inspector										
8. Opinion of pupils' parents										
9. Opinion of pupils themselves										

17.   In your work as a teacher, how far do you feel that your teaching practice is influenced by each of the following factors?

I am influenced by:	Degree of influence				
	Very strongly	Strongly	Only a little	Not at all	Does not concern me
1. My family background					
2. My initial training					
3. My personal teaching experience					
4. My own reading/independent study					
5. My colleagues at work					
6. My headteacher					
7. My school inspector					
8. My pupils					
9. Parents of my pupils					
10. My membership of a professional association					
11. My experience of specialist personal courses, e.g. encounter groups, assertiveness training					
12. My participation in extra-curricular activities with children					
13. My participation in in-service training					
14. My professional ideology					
15. My study for a university degree/diploma					
16. Other (please specify)					

Which of these influences is the most important for you?

_____

Which is the least important?

_____

18. What does 'professional responsibility' mean for you as a teacher?

_____

_____

_____

_____

_____

_____

_____

_____

_____

_____

19a. In general, how much freedom do you have to choose the content of your teaching?

Complete freedom ☐

A great deal of freedom ☐

Considerable freedom ☐

A little freedom ☐

Very little freedom
or no freedom at all ☐

19b. For what aspects of the curriculum do you feel you have the greatest freedom of choice?

_____

_____

19c. For what aspects of the curriculum do you feel you have the least freedom of choice?

_____

_____

19d. What are the major constraints which determine for you the content of your teaching?

_____

_____

20a.   In general, how much freedom do you have over the choice of teaching methods?

Complete freedom ☐

A great deal of freedom ☐

Considerable freedom ☐

A little freedom ☐

No freedom at all ☐

20b.   In what aspects of your teaching methods do you have the greatest freedom?

_____

_____

20c.   In what aspects of your teaching methods do you have the least freedom?

_____

_____

20d.   What are the major constraints which determine for you your teaching methods?

_____

_____

22.   Your work as a teacher can have short-term, medium-term and long-term outcomes. What are likely to be the most important outcomes of your own teaching for your pupils?

(a) In the short term, i.e. in the course of this school year?

_____

_____

(b) In the medium term, i.e. as they complete compulsory schooling?

_____

_____

(c) In the long term, i.e. when your pupils have become adults?

_____

_____

21. In your professional practice, how important is the responsibility you have for the following educational objectives?

Educational objective	Essential	Very important	Important	Important to some extent	Fairly unimportant	Not important at all
1. Actual instruction/academic work						
2. Development of the child's personality						
3. Training in personal relations						
4. Moral education						
5. Development of the intelligence						
6. Training of the future citizen						
7. Physical education						
8. Sex education						
9. Artistic/aesthetic education						
10. Health education						
11. Children's behaviour in class						
12. Arouse an interest in learning						
13. That children should enjoy what they are doing						
14. That children should like hard work and effort						
15. That children are kept constructively engaged						
16. That children see the relevance of what they are doing						
17. That pupils should be able to apply their knowledge in the future						
18. That children know how to organize their work						
19. Helping the child to become mature						

Which is the *most* essential of these objectives for you? (Give the number) _____

Which is the *least* essential of these objectives for you? _____

23.   For a teacher, to 'be responsible' also means to 'be accountable' to others. From this point of view, to whom and how much do you feel responsible?

To whom:	I feel:				
	Very responsible	Responsible	Responsible to some extent	Not very responsible	Not responsible at all
To yourself and your own conscience					
To your headteacher					
To the parents of your pupils					
To your school					
To your inspector					
To your colleagues					
To your pupils					
To society in general					

24.   Whether you feel more or less responsible, for what do you feel the most responsibility in relation to:

Yourself	
Your headteacher	
The parents	
Your school	
Your inspector	
Your colleagues	
Your pupils	
Society in general	

25. To what extent do you agree with each of the following statements?

	Strongly agree	Agree to some extent	Disagree to some extent	Don't agree at all
1. Parents should have a say in what their children learn at school				
2. It is up to teachers to decide, on the basis of their professional experience, what is best for the child				
3. A teacher's practice should follow the directions laid down by government policy				
4. It is a teacher's duty to explain the methods he or she is using to parents				
5. The teacher must adapt his or her methods to the social composition of the local area				
6. At the end of the day, teachers are only responsible to their own conscience				
7. Teachers' activities in the classroom must take into account the needs and the socio-economic characteristics of the local environment				
8. Teachers should adapt their teaching (curriculum and methods) to meet parents' wishes				
9. What teachers do from day to day should reflect the policy of the head				
10. Teachers should be available to discuss personal matters with parents				
11. A child's progress in school is not ultimately the responsibility of the teacher				
12. A teacher has a great deal of freedom in his or her professional practice				
13. Teachers should be ready to listen to parents' opinions				
14. The professional responsibility expected of a teacher depends in the last resort on the working conditions that the State provides				
15. The teacher has a great deal of freedom in the choice of teaching methods				
16. The teacher must adapt the content of her or his teaching to the social composition of the local area				
17. It is right that teachers should have to justify their classroom practice to those in authority over them				

26. In a few words, can you describe the essential elements of your teaching style?

_____

_____

_____

_____

27. How far do you agree with each of the following statements about the nature of teaching?

For me, teaching:	Agree completely	Agree to some extent	Disagree to some extent	Disagree completely
1. is a vocation				
2. is a means of earning a living like any other				
3. is collaboration in a creative endeavour with my colleagues				
4. is the daily pleasure of contact with children				
5. is a way of giving meaning to my life				
6. is a very hard job				
7. is a daily challenge				
8. is to do a job which is little valued by society				
9. gives me the chance of interesting social relationships				
10. means being isolated in my work				

C. PERSONAL DETAILS

28. In which age group are you?

30 or under	31–45	over 45
☐	☐	☐

29. How many years have you been a teacher?

under 5 years ☐ 11–20 years ☐
5–10 years ☐ over 20 years ☐

30. Please state your sex:

Male   Female

☐   ☐

31. How long have you worked in your present school? _____

32a. How far do you live from your school?

Less than 1 mile	☐
1–5 miles	☐
More than 5 miles	☐

b. How long on average does your journey to school take in the morning?

_____

33. Do you live:

Alone {	with children	☐
	without children	☐
With one or more other adults {	with children	☐
	without children	☐

34. Which of the following qualifications do you hold? Please tick all which apply

Certificate in Education	☐
BEd	☐
Postgraduate Certificate in Education	☐
Diploma in Advanced Studies in Education	☐
MEd	☐
Other – please specify	☐

35. You have just answered a questionnaire in which many of the questions have dealt with your professional responsibility. We are most grateful. Is there an important question which you have not been asked? If yes, what is it?

_____

_____

How would you reply to it?

_____

_____

Bibliography

Abric, J.C. (1976) Jeux, conflits et représentations sociales. Thèse de Doctorat d'État, Université de Provence.

Abric, J.C. (1984) A theoretical and experimental approach to the study of social representations in a situation of interaction. In R. Farr and S. Moscovici (eds) *Social Representations*. Cambridge: Cambridge University Press.

Acker, S. (1987) Primary school teaching as an occupation. In S. Delamont (ed.) *The Primary School Teacher*. Lewes: Falmer Press.

Acker, S. (1990) Teachers' culture in an English primary school: continuity and change. *BJSE*, **11**, 257–73.

Apple, M. (1986) *Teachers and Texts: A Political Economy of Class and Gender Relations in Education*. London: Routledge.

Archer, M. (1979) *The Social Origins of Educational Systems*. London: Sage.

Avon Council (1984) *Social Stress in Avon, a Preliminary Analysis*.

Avon Planning Office (1981) *Social Data in the Country of Avon*.

Ball, S. and Goodson, I. (eds) (1985) *Teachers' Lives and Careers*. Lewes: Falmer Press.

Barton, L. and Walker, S. (1985) *Education and Social Change*. London: Croom Helm.

Baudelot, C. and Establet, R. (1971) *L'école capitaliste en France*. Paris: Maspero.

Baudelot, C. and Establet, R. (1975) *L'école primaire divisé*. Paris: Maspero.

Becher, T. and Maclure, S. (1978) *The Politics of Curriculum Change*. London: Hutchinson.

Becher, T., Eraut, M. and Knight, J. (1981) *Policies for Educational Accountability*. London: Heinemann Educational.

Bell, R. and Grant, N. (1974) *A Mythology of British Education*. London: Panther.

Berger, I. (1979) *Les instituteurs d'une génération à l'autre*. Paris: Presses Universitaires de France.

Bernstein, B. (1977) *Class, Codes and Control*. London: Routledge & Kegan Paul.

Bertrand, A.J.C. (1966) *Le guide des instituteurs: législation, programmes, instructions officielles, adresses utiles*. Issygneux (Haute Loire): Imprimerie Moderne.

Bourdieu, P. (1979) Classement, déclassement, reclassement. *Actes de la Recherche en Sciences Sociales*, **24**.

Bourdieu, P. and Passeron, J.C. (1964) *Les héritiers, les étudiants et la culture*. Paris: Les Éditions de Minuit.

Bourdieu, P. and Passeron, J.C. (1970) *La reproduction: éléments pour une théorie du système d'enseignement*. Paris: Les Éditions de Minuit.

Bourdieu, P. and Passeron, J.C. (1977) *La réproduction*. Paris: Sage.

Broadfoot, P. (1977) Decision-making in education – the comparative contribution. *Comparative Education* special issue, Summer 1977, **13**(2), 133–7.

Broadfoot, P. (1981) Constants and contexts in educational accountability. Report to the SSRC, unpublished.

Broadfoot, P. (1982a) Accountability in England and France: the centralist alternative? *Education Policy Bulletin*, **10**(1).
Broadfoot, P. (1982b) Assessment constraints on curriculum practice: a comparative study. In M. Hammersley and A. Hargreaves (eds) *Curriculum Practice: Some Sociological Case Studies*. Lewes: Falmer Press.
Broadfoot, P. (1983) Education and the social order in advanced industrial societies: the educational dilemma. *International Review of Applied Psychology*, **32**, 307-25.
Broadfoot, P. (1985) Changing patterns of educational accountability in England and France. *Comparative Education*, **21**, 273-86.
Broadfoot, P. and Osborn, M. (1987) Teachers' conceptions of their professional responsibility: some international comparisons. *Comparative Education*, **23**(3), 287-301.
Broadfoot, P. and Osborn, M. (1988) What professional responsibility means to teachers: national contexts and classroom constants. *British Journal of Sociology of Education*, **7**(3), 265-87.
Broadfoot, P. and Osborn, M. (1992) French lessons: comparative perspectives on what it means to be a teacher. *Oxford Studies in Comparative Education*, **1**, 69-88.
Bulletin officiel de l'Éducation nationale (1990) *Une nouvelle politique pour l'école primaire*. 15 February 1990.
Bulletin officiel de l'Éducation nationale (1990) *Projet d'école*. 15 February 1990.
Burgess, R.G. (1984) *In the Field: An Introduction to Field Research*. London: Allen & Unwin.
Calderhead, J. (1987) *Exploring Teachers' Thinking*. London: Cassell.
Centre Départemental de Documentation Pédagogique de l'Essonne. *L'école dès 12*. France: Coulomb, C.; Grande Bretagne: Vieville, S.
Chapoulie, J.M. (1973) Sur l'analyse sociologique des groupes professionels. *Revue Française de Sociologie*, **13**, 11-20.
Chapoulie, J.M. (1974) Le corps professoral dans la structure de classe. *Revue Française de Sociologie*, **14**, 85-114.
Chapoulie, J.M. (1987) *Les professeurs de l'enseignement secondaire: un métier de classe moyenne*. Paris: Éditions de la Maison des Sciences de l'Homme.
Code Soleil (1982) 51 edition, Presses du Massif Central: SUDEL.
Cohen, L. and Manion, L. (1987) *Research Methods in Education*. London: Croom Helm.
Cox, C.B. and Dyson, A. (1969) *Fight for Education: A Black Paper*. London: The Critical Quarterly Society.
Crossley, M. and Vulliamy, G. (1984) Case study research methods and comparative education. *Comparative Education*, **20**, 193-207.
Crozier, M. (1964) *The Bureaucratic Phenomenon*. Chicago: University of Chicago Press.
David, M. (1977) *Reform, Reaction and Resources: The Three Rs of Educational Planning*. Slough: NFER.
DES (1977) *Education in Schools: A Consultative Document*. Green Paper, HMSO 6869.
DES (1978) *Assessing the Performance of Pupils*. Report on Education No. 93.
DES and Welsh Office (1977) *A New Partnership for Our Schools* (The Taylor Report). HMSO.
Direction de l'évaluation et de la prospective (1989) *Repères et references statistiques sur l'enseignement et la formation*. Ministère de l'Éducation Nationale et de la Jeunesse et des Sports, No. 18.
Duclaud-Williams, R. (1980) Teacher unions and educational policy in Britain and France. Paper presented to ECPR Workshop on Pressure Groups and the State, Florence.
Dujykes, H.C.J. and Rokkhan, S. (1954) Organisational aspects of cross-national social research. *Journal of Social Issues*, **10**, 8-24.
Durkheim, E. (1956) *Education and Society* (trans S.D. Fox). Chicago: Chicago Free Press.
Eaglesham, E. (1956) *From School Board to Local Authority*. London: Routledge.
Elliott, J. *et al.* (1981) *School Accountability*. Bury St Edmunds: Grant McIntyre.
Evans, A. (1977) Secondary education (editorial). *Education in Schools*, **7**(2), 13-17.
Fiske, D. (1982) Review. *Education*, 29 January, p. 29.
Fullan, M. (1991) *The New Meaning of Educational Change*. London: Cassell.
Furet, F. and Ozouf, J. (1977) *Lire et écrire: l'alphabétisation des Français de Calvin à Jules Ferry*. Paris: Les Éditions de Minuit.
Geddes, B. (1982) Pupil self-assessment: theoretical and practical issues. University of Bristol: MEd thesis.

Gilly, M. (1967) Influence du milieu social et de l'âge sur la progression scolaire à l'école primaire. *Bulletin de Psychologie*, **20**, 797–810.

Gilly, M. (1969) *Bon élève – mauvais élève: recherche sur les déterminants des différences de réussite scolaire à conditions égales d'intelligence et de milieu social*. Paris: A. Colin.

Gilly, M. (1972a) La représentation de l'élève par le maître à l'école primaire: coherence entre aspects structuraux et différentials: *Cahiers de Psychologie*, **15**, 201–16.

Gilly, M. (1972b). Représentation des finalités de l'école primaire par des péres de famille: première contribution. *Cahiers de Psychologie*, **15**, 227–38 (in collaboration with M. Paillard).

Gilly, M. (1980) *Maître-élève: rôles institutionnels et représentations*. Paris: Presses Universitaires de France.

Gilly, M. (1984) Psychosociologie de l'éducation. In S. Moscovici (ed.) *Psychologie sociale*. Paris: Presses Universitaires de France, pp. 473–95.

Gilly, M. (1989) Les représentations sociales dans le champ educatif. In D. Jodelet (ed) *Les représentations sociales*. Paris: Presses Universitaires de France, pp. 362–86.

Hammersley, M. (1980) Putting competence into action: some sociological notes on a model of classroom interaction. In P. French and M. Maclure (eds) *Adult–Child Conversation*. London: Croom Helm.

Hargreaves, A. (1984) Experience counts: theory doesn't: how teachers talk about their work. *Sociology of Education*, **57**, 244–54.

Hargreaves, A. (1986) Teaching quality: a sociological analysis. *J. Curriculum Studies*, **20**(3), 211–31.

Hargreaves, D. (1988) Educational research and the implications of the 1988 Educational Reform Act. Lecture given to BERA Annual Conference, University of East Anglia.

Hoskin, K. (1977) The examination, disciplinary powers and rational schooling. *History of Education*, **8**(2), 135–46.

Hoyle, E. (1973) *The Study of Schools as Organisations*. Bristol: University of Bristol, School of Education.

Hoyle, E. (1980) Professionalisation and deprofessionalisation in education. In E. Hoyle and J. Megarry (eds) *World Yearbook of Education 1980: Professional Development of Teachers*. London: Kogan Page, pp. 42–54.

Institut National de la Statistique et des Études Économiques (INSEE) (1978) *Données Sociales*.

Isambert-Jamati, V. (1984) *Culture, technique et critique sociale à l'école élémentaire*. Paris: Presses Universitaires de France.

Jackson, P. W. (1968) *Life in Classrooms*. Chicago: Holt, Rinehart & Winston.

Johnson, D., Ransom, E., Packwood, T., Bowden, K. and Kogan, M. (1980) *Secondary Schools and the Welfare Network*. London: Allen & Unwin.

Johnson, N. (1980) *In Search of the Constitution: Reflections on State and Society in Britain*. London: Methuen.

Keddie, N. (1971) Classroom knowledge. In M. Young (ed.) *Knowledge and Control*. London: Macmillan.

Kogan, M. (1984) Education accountability: an analytic overview prepared for the ESRC. Department of Government, Brunel University.

Lawn, M. and Ozga, J. (1981) The educational worker: a reassessment of teachers. In J. Ozga (ed) *Schoolwork: Approaches to the Labour Process of Teaching*. Milton Keynes: Open University Press.

Leger, A. (1980) Situation et position sociales des professeurs en France. Thèse de 3me cycle, Université Paris 5 (René Descartes).

Leger, A. (1982) Enseignants, stratégie de carrière et alliance avec la classe ouvrière. *Societé Française, Cahiers de l'Institut de Recherches Marxistes*, **2**, 30–5.

Lerner, D. (1956) Interviewing Frenchmen. *American Journal of Sociology*, **62**, 193.

Litt, E. and Parkinson, M. (1979) *US and UK Educational Policy: A Decade of Reform*. New York: Praeger.

McIntyre, D. (gen. ed. W. Inglis) (1977) *What Responsibility Should Teachers Accept?* Paper No. 1, University of Stirling, Department of Education.

MacPherson, G. (1972) *Small Town Teacher*. Cambridge, MA: Harvard University Press.

Menlo, A. and Poppleton, P. (1990) A five country study of the work perceptions of secondary school teachers in England, the US, Japan, Singapore and West Germany. *Comparative Education*, **26**(2/3), 173–83.

Morrison, A. and McIntyre, D. (1975) *Profession: enseignant. Une psychosociologie de l'enseignant* (trans. M. Linard) Paris: A. Colin.

Mugny, G. and Carugati, F. (1985) *L'intelligence au pluriel: les représentations sociales de l'intelligence et de son développement*. Éditions de Val.

Munn, P., Hewitt, G., Morrison, A. and McIntyre, D. (1982) *Accountability and Professionalism*. Stirling Educational Monographs 10.

Neave, G. (1988) On the cultivation of quality, efficiency and enterprise: and overview of recent trends in higher education in Western Europe, 1986–1988. *European Journal of Education*, **23**(1/2), 7–24.

Nias, J. (1986) What it is to feel like a teacher. Paper given at a symposium on 'Becoming and Being a Teacher', Bristol: BERA Conference.

Nias, J. (1989) *Primary Teachers Talking: A Study of Teaching as Work*. London: Routledge.

Nias, J., Southworth, G. and Yeomans, R. (1989) *Staff Relationships in the Primary School: A Study of Organizational Cultures*. London: Cassell.

Osborn, M. and Broadfoot, P. (1987) French lessons: what comparative research can teach us about plans for a national curriculum. *Times Educational Supplement*, 3 July.

Osborn, M. and Broadfoot, P. (1992a) A lesson in progress? Primary classrooms observed in England and France. *Oxford Review of Education*, **18**(1), 3–15.

Osborn, M. and Broadfoot, P., with Abbott, D., Croll, P. and Pollard, A. (1992b) The impact of current changes in English primary schools on teacher professionalism. *Teachers College Record*, **94**(1), 138–51.

Osborn, M. and Pollard, A. (1990) Anxiety and paradox: teachers' initial responses to change under the National Curriculum. PACE Working Paper No. 3.

Parry, N. and Parry, J. (1981) The teachers and professionalism: the failure of an occupational strategy. In Dale *et al.* (eds) *Education and the State*, vol. 3. Lewes: Falmer Press.

Perie, R. (1989) *L'éducation nationale à l'heure de la décentralisation*. Paris: La Documentation Française.

Phillips, D. (1989) Neither a borrower nor a lender be? The problems of cross-national attraction in education. *Comparative Education*, **25**(3), 267–74.

Pollard, A., Broadfoot, P., Croll, P., Osborn, M. and Abbott, D. (1994) *Changing English Primary Schools: The Impact of the Education Reform Act at Key Stage 1*. London: Cassell.

Poppleton, P. (1986) The experience of teaching in disadvantaged areas in the UK and USA. Paper given at a symposium on 'Becoming and Being a Teacher'. Bristol: BERA Conference.

Poppleton, P. (1990) The significance of being alike: the implications of similarities and differences in the work-perceptions of teachers in an international five country study. *Comparative Education*, **29**(2), 215–23.

Powell, V. (1985) *The Teacher's Craft*. Edinburgh: SCRE.

Prost, A. (1968) *Histoire de l'enseignement en France 1899–1967*. Paris: A. Colin.

Salter, B. and Tapper, T. (1981) *Education, Politics and the State*. London: Grant-McIntyre.

Selltiz, C., Jahoda, M., Deutsch, M. and Cook, S. W. (1965) *Research Methods in Social Relations*. London: Methuen.

Sharp, R. and Green, A. (1975) *Education and Social Control*. London: Routledge & Kegan Paul.

Silver, H. (1979) Accountability in education: towards a history of some English features. Paper for SSRC Panel on Accountability in Education, London.

Silver, H. (1980) *Education and the Social Condition*. London: Methuen.

Simon, B. (1960) *Studies in the History of Education 1800–1870*. London: Lawrence & Wishart.

Simon, B. (1965) *Education and the Labour Movement 1870–1920*. London: Routledge & Kegan Paul.

Sockett, H., Bailey, C., Bridges, D., Elliott, J., Gibson, R., Scrimshaw, P. and White, J. (eds) (1984) *Accountability in the English Education System*. London: Hodder & Stoughton.

Sutherland, G. (1977) The magic of measurement: mental testing in English education 1900–1940. *Transactions of the Royal Historical Society*, 135–53.

Voluzan, J. (1975) *L'école primaire jugée: fonctionnement pédagogique de l'école primaire*. Paris: Librairie Larousse.

Warwick, D. and Osherson, S. (eds) (1973) *Comparative Research Methods: An Overview*. Englewood Cliffs, NJ: Prentice-Hall.

Webb, R.B. and Ashton, P.T. (1987) Teacher motivation and the conditions for teaching. In
    S. Walker and L. Barton (eds) *Changing Policies, Changing Teachers*. Milton Keynes: Open
    University Press.
Weiler, H. (1988) Reform politics in French education. *Comparative Education Review*, 32(3),
    251–66.
Woods, P. (1986) *Inside Schools: Ethnography in Educational Research*. London: Routledge &
    Kegan Paul.

Name Index

Abbott, D. (Pollard *et al.*) 102
Abric, J.C. 15
Acker, S. 8, 9
Apple, M. 120
Archer, M. 26
Ashton, P.T. 10, 126–7
Avon Planning Office 43

Bailey, C. (Sockett *et al.*) 122
Ball, S. 9
Becher, T. 29, 119
Bell, R. 25
Bernstein, B. 123
Bourdieu, P. 3, 11, 14
Bridges, D. (Sockett *et al.*) 122
Broadfoot, P. 3, 8, 10, 15, 33, 36, 38,
    (Pollard *et al.*) 102, 124, 126
Burgess, R.G. 47

Calderhead, J. 12
Cohen, L. 44
Cook, S.W. (Selltiz *et al.*) 44
Cox, C.B. 30
Croll, P. (Pollard *et al.*) 102
Crossley, M. 10, 49
Crozier, M. 8

David, M. 29
Deutsch, M. (Selltiz *et al.*) 44
Duclaud-Williams, R. 39
Dujykes, H.J.C. 48
Durkheim, E. 8–9, 14
Dyson, A. 30

Eaglesham, E. 26

Elliott, J. 119, (Sockett *et al.*)
    122

Fullan, M. 127
Furet, F. 18, 20

Geddes, B. 126
Gibson, R. (Sockett *et al.*) 122
Gilly, M. 12–13, 67, 68
Goodson, I. 9
Grant, N. 25
Green, A. 3, 11, 125

Hammersley, M. 123
Hargreaves, A. 14, 91, 123
Hewitt, G. (Munn *et al.*) 119
Hoskin, K. 121
Hoyle, E. 79, 104, 120

Institut National de la Statistique et des Études
    Économiques (INSEE) 19, 43
Isambert-Jamati, V. 3, 11, 14

Jackson, P.W. 91
Jahoda, M. (Selltiz *et al.*) 44
Johnson, N. 26

Keddie, N. 125
Kogan, M. 119–20

Lawn, M. 120

Subject Index